FALLING
THROUGH FIRE

CLIFFORD THOMPSON

Mirror Books

Published by Mirror Books,
an imprint of Trinity Mirror plc,
1 Canada Square,
London E14 5AP, England

www.mirrorbooks.com
twitter.com/themirrorbooks

ISBN 978-1-907324-70-3

First paperback edition

**Names, dates and identifying details have been changed to
protect the privacy of individuals**

Printed and bound in Great Britain
by CPI Group (UK) Ltd, Croydon, CR0 4YY

CONTENTS

Clifford Thompson is a journalist, writer and former London Firefighter.

He has worked in television news for more than 20 years and is a staff journalist with BBC News covering national and international stories.

He has a Diploma of Higher Education in psychology from the University of East London, a BA (hons) degree from the University of London (Birkbeck) in Humanities and in 2012, he graduated from City University's MA in narrative non-fiction writing with a distinction.

In 2014 he was awarded a scholarship by the Norman Mailer Center in the US, at the University of Utah to study creative non-fiction and develop his writing. The venue was Salt Lake City – the setting for Mailer's The Executioner's Song.

Falling Through Fire is his first book – a memoir about his time, first as a firefighter, then as a journalist working on major disasters including the 1993 World Trade Center bombing and the Paddington train crash.

For Monika

Prologue
Hackney 1990

The sun was setting over Hackney, East London, on a muggy summer's evening. The air was heavy and there was a buzz in the atmosphere. It was a rough area, riddled with crime and poverty, where tension often filled the streets. The Blue Watch at Kingsland Road fire station was on the night shift. Just over three hours had passed since their duties began at six that evening; there were still 12 to go.

Kingsland was about a mile to the east of Bishopsgate, in the City of London. Firefighters were scattered all over the station; some chatted in the locker room, the mess manager was preparing supper in the kitchen on the first floor, while the officers were busy completing reports from fires earlier in the week.

I was 23 years old, and this was only my fourth shift at Kingsland, having recently transferred from Stratford a few miles to the east. On my second shift I'd been offered temporary promotion, and was now an acting leading firefighter with five years' experience under my belt.

Darkness fell. At 22:09 the call bells rang. Conversations stopped and chores were abandoned as the fire crews mustered in the appliance bay, then climbed into the trucks.

'Everyone on?' shouted my driver, Ray, above the noise of angry revving engines.

We eased through the appliance bay doors to a chorus of

sirens. The noise sent pigeons flapping into the air, froze pedestrians to the spot, and warned drivers to clear a path on the road. The three fire engines – the pump ladder, the pump and the hydraulic platform turned left on the way to the council estate. We never called them engines; we called them machines.

Flashes of blue bounced from glass shopfronts, lighting up the cab of the pump ladder. Behind me, separated by an open plate-metal bulkhead, my crew fastened on tunics and strapped into the harnesses of their breathing apparatus with cries of 'What we got?' and 'I hope supper isn't fucked.'

Our destination was the sprawling 1970s Holly Street council estate in Hackney, also known as 'the snake' for its row of housing blocks each connected by an open landing. Home to thousands of people, the estate was rife with crime, drugs and prostitution. At its eastern edge rose four tower blocks: Rowan, Lomas, Grange and Cedar Courts. They were designed to be built quickly, assembled panel-by-panel, each block a 20-storey architectural kit dominating the skyline.

As we turned into the estate, the officer-in-charge, riding the front of the pump, sent a coded message on the main radio channel: 'M-2-F-E – Foxtrot three-one-one, Foxtrot three-one-two and Foxtrot three-one-four – all status three. Over,' telling the control room we had arrived.

I climbed from my machine's cab and, with the other two officers, looked up at Cedar Court. There was a fire raging on the 13th floor.

'Get the keys to the dry-riser box door, breathing apparatus crew to the lift, take a couple of lengths of hose and a branch,' the station officer ordered the firefighters as they flew into action. The driver of Kingsland's pump connected a length of hose from a hydrant in the street to one of the trucks; another was rolled out from the truck to the dry-riser inlet outside the tower block. Lockers on the trucks flew open as firefighters took ropes, an extinguisher and a sledge-hammer. My crew, wearing breathing apparatus but with face masks hanging around their necks, headed for the lifts. Gusts of black smoke flew into the dimming cobalt sky, as bursts of flames rose against the façade of the block. This is what we'd call a working job: a serious fire that required crews to get to work. Rubbish burning in a bin would not be classified as a working job. But one where you can see someone needs help, and what you're doing impacts on someone else – that's a working job.

I was in charge of Kingsland's pump ladder, which carried rescue and cutting equipment, breathing apparatus as well as a pump and tank of water. My men were responsible for rescue, and were the first to enter the burning flat, taking the lift a hundred feet above ground ahead of me. Stopping on the floor below, they climbed the stairs to the smoke-filled landing and the burning flat. The station officer and I entered the lobby and were about to take the lift when a man, looking agitated, suddenly appeared.

'There's a body – on the ground. It's around the back!' He spat out the words, his voice filled with breathless panic.

'Get round there, Cliff!' the governor shouted. 'Make pumps four – persons reported,' he said, instructing one of the drivers to send a priority radio message and request additional pumps.

Six miles away, an officer in the headquarters control room in Lambeth dispatched more crews from neighbouring stations Homerton and Shoreditch, bringing the total to four. We called these fires 'make-ups', another name for a working job. A 'persons reported' meant someone was missing, trapped or unaccounted for, so an ambulance and the police were also called by the control officer.

Such jobs were very common. Some escalated to six, eight, 10, 15, 20 and 25 pumpers involving hundreds of firefighters. A job that was well alight was described by firefighters as going like a bastard, and it was these fires that we loved the most.

I ran out of the lobby and around the outside of the tower block, and discovered another man, a little dishevelled, standing on a quilt covering what looked like a body.

'Someone's jumped – he's fucking dead. Help!' he yelled. Despite his distress he frantically tried to light a cigarette. He shook violently, keeping one foot on the quilt, trying to protect what was underneath from onlookers.

With me were only two of the Blue Watch firefighters. The humidity was occasionally eased by gusts of wind blowing through the gaps between the tower blocks, causing the quilt to flap in violent bursts. The air was sticky as the summer day faded into night. A crowd gathered: young, old, black and white. Some looked, then looked away. Their shock was palpable.

'Can we have a salvage sheet?' I asked, and one of my crew, Dave, ran around the block to the pump ladder. My priority was to keep the growing crowd under control since 'the snake' was prone to erupt, and uniforms were rarely welcome. 'Get back! Move! Give us some space!' I shouted. Dave returned with the tarpaulin salvage sheet and began to unfold it. I pulled back the tatty quilt under which lay a body, spread-eagled and looking like a leopard skin rug. I moved closer and saw the glassy-eyed stare of a lifeless human being.

I reached for my personal radio hanging from my fire tunic, and called up the governor who was supervising the firefighting operation on the 13th floor.

'It's fatal, guv. We've got a body. Over.'

The radio crackled with static as he replied: 'Send an informative message from me to control: flat on 13th floor, five meters by eight metres, 75% alight, one jet, breathing apparatus in use, one person apparently dead before arrival of brigade. Request attendance of police and confirm the fire investigation team and brigade photographer are mobile. Over.'

'All received. Over.' I called to Ray, who was operating the pump, its whirring impeller pushing thousands of gallons of water up the tower block: 'Send this message in the guv's name.' Ray tore the sheet from my notebook, the message written with a pencil in shorthand.

I bent over the body and felt for a pulse – a matter of routine and respect, but with five years' experience of fighting fires in East London, I knew what a dead body looked like: vacant eyes, locked in a fixed gaze, limp limbs that would stiffen with rigor mortis in the next couple of hours. The skin was sickly pale, hair dark, and there was blood running from the mouth, ears, nose, and between the legs. Fixed on the victim's face was an expression of horror. It was impossible to know if the person was male or female.

It was an undignified and brutal death. We removed the quilt and covered the body with the salvage sheet to give some degree of respect. The force of the victim's exit from the flat on the 13th floor had carried them away from the tower block, hitting an area of scruffy grass nearby. Death was instant, but the body remained intact, face down, head tilted up and looking straight ahead. Had it landed differently on concrete, the body would have shattered, spilling blood, fat and body parts over a wider area.

'Anyone know this person?' I asked the crowd. A few people shrugged their shoulders. Some turned away.

I took notes to help prepare a report later when we returned to the station.

High above ground, the grey block now covered in thick, sooty streaks, the fire was brought under control, supervised by the governor.

'Any chance you can tell me the victim's gender?' I asked one of the paramedics.

'Yeah, no worries, mate.' He lifted up the salvage sheet and checked by pushing his hands between the legs of the body. 'It's a man. Definitely a man.'

We discovered later that the fire hadn't killed him. He was a Chinese student, who had lit a cigarette and drifted off to sleep after taking some medication that made him drowsy. Even the flames spreading through the lounge didn't rouse him, and the carbon monoxide released in the smoke confused him further.

Much later, his death was fully investigated by the police and an inquest opened. For my report, completed after the fire, I concluded that the man had eventually woken up, but was completely disorientated by the spreading fire, smoke and the effects of the pills he'd taken. He bolted through the door onto the flat's balcony, moving with such force that he fell over the waist-high ledge to his death. With no witness or second person discovered in the fire, we were never sure of his exact motive, but pieced together the facts from the little information we had. If only he'd stayed on the balcony in the fresh air until we arrived and waited, he probably would have lived.

We returned to the station, cleaned our kit, had a cup of tea and wrote up our reports. The station was filled with noise: an ancient manual typewriter ticked away in the station office, an entry was logged on the register of calls, compiled in triplicate with sheets of inky carbon copy paper. The clack of off-white crockery and worn stainless-steel cutlery came from the mess upstairs – it was nearly time for supper. There was excited banter along the corridor in the locker room from some of the Blue Watch firefighters, and the ringing of full compressed-air cylinders knocking against each other as they were swapped by my crew with those used at the fire on the back of the pump ladder.

Four hours of the night shift had passed. There were 11 to go.

Two weeks after that fire, my family gathered for my cousin's wedding. I told the story of the spread-eagled body many times that day. I was matter-of-fact about it ('It's just what we do') but knew that some found the tale too shocking.

Being a firefighter meant having a view of the world that most people didn't experience. There was a great tradition of gathering in the mess after a job and recounting events, often with added commentary or colour. I'd take those stories away and share them. My confidence grew and I enjoyed being the centre of attention, occasionally boasting about my latest experience to friends or family.

Death was, by now, routine. I felt immune from its effects and had been to hundreds of incidents protected by the other firefighters, our equipment, my skill and experience. We'd have a couple of beers in the pub before a night shift (drinking had once even been allowed on duty), and if it was quiet, I'd often sleep for six or seven hours if the bells didn't go down. I had a large disposable income, busy social life and enjoyed lots of dates. I had also developed a method to cope with the disasters I encountered, transferring each one to a mental filing system. Any tragedy became a record card, tucked away in the back of my mind. The events of the previous tour of duty were just clipped entries, written in a small week-to-view diary.

Firefighters don't enjoy seeing people in pain and especially dislike seeing children suffer or die. These are the worst incidents, the ones that subdue the entire watch, bring a sense of loss to the crews involved, and make them search deep within for an answer. But in five years, I had not experienced the death of a child.

Otherwise, firefighters crave the next working job, boasting among themselves about the role they played in the action and drama. They laugh at what to the outsider might seem inappropriate or unspeakable. No one claims to be a hero – they leave that for others to say – but most yearn to play that role and love being in the grip of a crisis. The more extreme the fire, the more complex the rescue, the more they love it. It's an addiction: to the gruesome and the bizarre, fuelled by adrenaline, and it starts the very first time the bells sound. They are worshipped the world over.

When firefighters stop loving what they do, they might move to a quiet fire station or take a less demanding role at the training centre in the fire-safety department..

By 1990, I was at the height of my own addiction to an adrenaline surge triggered by the ringing bells and speed of the machines. I was hooked on the flashing blue lights, yearned to get high on heat and smoke. If I could have paid for the next fix, I would have.

I felt untouchable, bulletproof and indestructible, and thought my trip would never end.

PART ONE: Beginnings
London, 1985 to 1992

Yea, though I walk through the valley
of the shadow of death
I will fear no evil, for thou art with me.
Thy road and thy staff, they comfort me...

23rd Psalm, King James Bible

CHAPTER 1

Inside The Triangle of Fire

It was 9am on 26 November 1985, and I was starting my first shift. I had just turned 19.

'So you're the new boy? Put your fire rig on. Be ready for roll call at 9 o'clock, son, OK?'

My voice cracked. 'OK.'

Mick was in his early 40s, with gingery hair and a soft and friendly manner, like a reassuring giant. I watched, listened to, and felt every tick of the clock as the seconds counted down. The locker room was full of banter from the other firefighters. I was surrounded by strangers who I would soon rely on as my role models and mates, every man the next link in my lifeline. One day, they would rely on me. They polished their fire boots by lockers as doors swung open, some displaying page-three pin-ups. The duty man rummaged in his for a necktie. He wore formal blue-black or 'undress' trousers, the same as the four officers: station officer, who also wore a white shirt with black epaulettes and black tie; sub officer, and two leading firemen who dressed separately in the junior officers' room. The rest of the watch wore light-blue 'workwear' trousers, black slip-on or lace-up leather shoes, and a light-blue collared shirt without a tie.

I was full of fear, excitement and anticipation, and felt like I weighed a ton. It was the first time I'd met my Red Watch workmates, my new family, who would guide me through life on the fire station and the fire ground.

There were four watches: Red, Blue, Green and White, with each watch, at that time, working a four-shift tour of duty: two days, two nights, four leave. Four watches ensures that every hour of each day is covered across London.

I had no real fire experience. My 20 weeks of training had finished a week before and now I was a firefighter in the London Fire Brigade (LFB), at that time the world's third-largest fire service with 114 stations. I was expected to learn fast and pull my weight.

Suddenly there sounded the short blasts on the station bells, which I counted to myself: one, two, three, four, five, six. Six bells, the code for 'all hands', summoning the Red Watch to the muster bay, a short corridor that led from the bottom of the pole-house – the vertical steel pole that enables firefighters to get from the first to the ground floor quickly – past the watch room where emergency calls were received, to the appliance bay and the parked machines (or fire engines) with their doors open, poised: the pump ladder, pump and hose-laying lorry. There were racks of fire rig in the muster bay that belonged to the off-duty watches: helmets, fire-boots, yellow overtrousers and tunics, redolent of stale smoke from previous jobs.

Six bells dismissed the Green Watch after their 48-hour tour of duty: two nine-hour days, then two 15-hour nights. Those firefighters going off duty went home between shifts.

We lined up wearing our fire rig, my glossy yellow helmet lacking the chips and knocks of the others. My tunic, tightly packed wool that smelled baby-fresh, was immaculate. The basic protective clothing had hardly changed for decades and was stored in the open so the strong smell didn't taint the clean uniform, which was kept in lockers.

'Red Watch: watch 'shun!' ordered the station officer. He turned to the sub officer: 'Call the roll!' he snapped with military precision.

'Answer your names: Leading Fireman Jones, Leading Fireman Nugent, Fireman Lewinton, Fireman Utley...'

The sub officer, who was second-in-command, read from a metal board with 16 names printed on paper, covered in thick clear plastic overwritten with a chinagraph pencil. He was a former sailor and looked every bit the part, the slashed peak of his cap pushed over his eyes so it almost touched his nose.

'Sir!' replied the men as their names were called. Eventually he got to me.

'Firefighter Thompson.'

'Sir!' I replied.

'What's your name, son?' asked the Sub Officer.

'Thompson, sir!'

I was not prepared for the informality of station life compared with training school.

Smiling, he asked again. 'It's OK. Your first name, son. What do we call you?'

'Cliff, sir!' I replied. The parading Red Watch laughed. I was now the junior buck or JB, fire-slang for the newest crew member to join the watch, a nickname that sticks until the arrival of the next recruit from training centre.

For the first six months I would ride the pump. Its main function was to supply water to a fire and attend routine emergencies, including special services – any incident that was not a fire, such as when people were shut in lifts or locked out of their houses, flooded buildings or rubbish and car fires. After six months under the watchful eye of the station officer, I would be allowed to ride the pump ladder, the primary function of which was rescue. Its crew put on breathing apparatus

(BA) en route to a fire call, leaving the face mask hanging down and the air supply shut off. They would only 'start up' their BA if they were going into a burning building.

Confusingly, both types of machine were known as pumping appliances. They held water in a tank, and used a hydrant to relay water to a fire from the street, to the machine, and then to the fire ground via a high-pressure pump.

At the end of roll call the governor made some announcements and our plans for the day were outlined.

'Red Watch: watch 'shun! To your duties. Fall out.'

That nervous, expectant feeling stayed with me all day, and for many shifts in those early months. Every ring of a phone, or the tinny clicking from the small bells that rang when a message was sent over the teleprinter, in the watch room; even the front doorbell caused an involuntary spasm and my heart to race. I'd go through the routine of what I'd do if the bells went down, and fought hard to hide my nerves from the others.

In the afternoon, the bells did go down and the pump was sent to a tower block in the E15. The call was to a person shut in a lift at James Riley Point, a tower block off Carpenters Road. It was my first taste of tearing through the traffic with two-tone horns wailing. It was a routine job. We wound the lift car down from the 10th floor to the seventh. I was in the motor room on the roof of the block and brought the lift compartment level with the landing, so the man could be released. It was a small milestone.

Stratford Fire Station is in the London Borough of Newham – one of England's most deprived areas. In 1985 the station's 'ground' had at its core a shopping centre, and two investment banks in high-rise blocks, surrounded by a busy one-way traffic system. It was a major rail junction for passengers and goods, and a large area was occupied by the London International Freight Terminal, where cargo arrived and departed in steel containers.

A new member of a watch was expected to learn the station's topography and build up a mental map of every building, station, river, canal and railway line, as well as the risks they posed, and the correct procedure for any type of incident.

Stratford had terraced houses and vast council estates with both high- and low-rise blocks with long, open landings. There was crime, and poverty, with scores of derelict warehouses and acres of redundant land, much of it polluted and scattered with addicts' needles. My ground, which was so diverse, gradually became familiar to me, shoehorned as it was between the bustle of the East End and the plains and furze at the southern tip of Epping Forest, where inner London collides with suburbia.

From my second shift, until I got the hang of it, I shadowed the duty man looking after the watch room, learning the procedure for when an emergency call came in, which was performed with military precision. Every firefighter on the watch took his turn being on duty in the watch room – 'being in the box' as it was called – and their job was to dispatch the crews and appliances when an emergency call came.

The language of firefighting is complicated with information conveyed in a mix of formal orders, shorthand, code and slang. Calls were received on antique teleprinters that had been in use since World War II and were about the size of a cooker hob. The teleprinter stood on a desk, and inside its gunmetal-grey cabinet was a high-speed typewriter carriage.

Routine messages, sent from the control room, were

accompanied by a green light and flat-sounding bell to summon the duty man. The carriage made a high-speed clicking noise as it moved automatically from left to right, and the entire watch would tense in anticipation. If it was an emergency call, the carriage travelled across a continuous role of four-ply paper and when it reached the middle, the house bells – or 'J-bells' – rang around the station. All the ceiling lights came on, along with a red light on top of the printer.

The duty man would go to the watch room, read out the call-slip with the incident details and tear off the top layers, which were given to the officers. A permanent paper record remained on the printer, and simply disappeared behind the back of the desk, a long stream of fire-service consciousness. At midnight, the duty man tore it off and rolled it up – a narrative of the day's events that was placed in a box. Messages giving updates from officers at incidents were sent by radio, then typed up by control officers. We were the only station in our area which was mobilised from a control room based on the same site as our fire station. There were also control rooms at Croydon and Wembley where 999 calls were received.

When a call came in, the duty man looked at the grid reference given on the teleprinter call slip and shouted it out to the drivers and officers in charge of the machines. An experienced motor driver knew every single road on his or her station's ground, knowledge that only came with experience. Their fire-gear was kept in a locker on the machine, and they rigged on arrival at the job as it was impossible to drive in the cumbersome tunic, boots and overtrousers. The rest of the crews went straight to their machines, putting their fire boots on then climbing on to the back of the engines.

The duty man turned on the different-coloured ceiling

lights to indicate which appliances were to be dispatched: red for the pump ladder, green for the pump, both lights if it was 'the pair'. A considerate duty man would shout 'Pump only!' in the night when that was the case, to save the others from rushing from their slumber. He would catch up with the rest of his crew, the last to jump on the pump ladder.

There was also a third blue light at Stratford for the hose-laying lorry. This truck, its officer and driver crew covered a significant part of London, an area much bigger than just Stratford's ground, as the brigade only had a handful of them. It was turned out frequently and attended calls to 'an alarm actuating' some miles away at the Ford Motor Company, the massive plant in Dagenham where the Cortina was built. There was only one risk on Stratford's ground to which 'all three' would turn out together: the London International Freight Terminal, which, more than 25 years later, following several billion pounds of investment, would become the Olympic Park, making Stratford famous the world over as London hosted the games for the third time in 2012.

At the start of a shift, after parading for roll call, the watch went upstairs to the mess for tea, and worked out the catering arrangements while chatting around a line of long tables. Many of the Red Watch smoked: some roll-ups, others tailor-made cigarettes. They smoked in the mess and the television room, but never in the station office or the watch room. After a job, they would gather at the back of the machines, and even though they'd come out of a fire, would discreetly light up.

On my second shift, I was given a 'practice' log book and I trailed the duty man watching, listening and learning. The log recorded the routine of the watch on duty, a handwritten and permanent record of sickness and lateness of firefighters, and the movement of the machines in every circumstance except an emergency. Those details were recorded on the teleprinter. It was updated with the names and changes of crew members, and listed details about a machine taken off-the-run or out of service.

My new life on the fire station revolved around learning the routine, which involved inspecting, checking and recording every detail about our equipment, no matter how trivial it seemed.

If a watch or firefighter was investigated for a disciplinary matter, the logbook was confiscated so the station's routine could be analysed.

Shifts were filled with training, drills, lectures and reading operational notes. I learned how things were done by repetition and asking questions, eventually accumulating a vast knowledge of Stratford's ground including every building and the risks posed. We went out on the pump, testing hydrants in the street, and inspected premises. I was expected to be the first to get to work, to keep busy and not question any orders from the officers or watch members. It took until just before Christmas for me to be competent enough to man the watch room alone.

Having made it through my first two day shifts, where nothing beyond routine happened, I reported for my first night shift on 28 November. We were allowed to sleep from midnight until 6.30am, unofficially until seven. It was Mick who spoke to me again shortly after supper finished at nine that night.

'Have you made your bed up, son? Get it done by around half-eleven, otherwise you'll have to do it later in the dark and disturb the whole watch.'

The dormitory on the ground floor was the size of

a hospital ward, with low black iron beds, each with a thin mattress. There were small widows above the beds at head height. We were issued with a single sheet not big enough to be tucked under the mattress, with four short strings to tie it to the bed frame; two horsehair blankets and a pillow. I had no top sheet to cover me so slept in my T-shirt against the coarse fibres of the 'horse' blanket. Trousers and shoes were laid out so they could be pulled on quickly when the bells rang, and shoes slipped into for the few seconds it took to run to the machines. There they'd be replaced with rubber fire boots and yellow polyurethane overtrousers.

It was the early hours of the morning and I couldn't sleep, so I got up and sat in the dark locker room adjacent to the dormitory. Mick joined me. 'What's the matter, son? Can't sleep?'

It felt like the longest night of my life. I felt disorientated, nervous, weary and confused, but was craving action. Stratford was a busy station but not that night.

'Don't worry, go upstairs to the mess and make a cuppa.'

In the early hours my boredom was broken by a call to another person stuck in a lift. I was pleased that I'd been on another emergency call, but I was desperate to go to a fire.

At eight in the morning, we ate a fried breakfast in the mess after washing the machines and tidying up.

On day shifts, we had a break known as 'stand easy' at 11 in the morning, which by tradition included cheese and raw onion sandwiches, and sausage with shiny fried onion sandwiches, with tea. Another tradition maintained at each station was the nutty locker that contained chocolate bars bought in bulk, soft drinks, razor blades and packets of painkillers. Each watch was responsible for its own nutty locker and when supplies ran down, cash was collected and the locker topped-up with a visit to a wholesaler. In the military, its equivalent would be the Navy Army and Air Force Institutes, or NAAFI, generally a separate building on a military base.

We had cooked lunches with a suet pudding and custard, plus afternoon tea, and probably consumed around seven or eight thousand calories on a day shift. But lots of food was essential due to the physically demanding nature of the job, and even when it was quiet I burned off the calories through nervous energy.

Our meals were lovingly prepared by Brenda, the station cook, a large Northern lady in her 60s, with loose, curly grey hair and a chubby round face, neatly made up.

Two day shifts had passed, and now one night shift. When six bells sounded at 9am, I went home and slept for a couple of hours, exhausted from doing nothing, but ready for the next night shift.

Fire fascinates me. As a teenage boy growing up in the 1970s, I remember the rich, woody smell of leaves burning in the late autumn chill by the edge of the road where we lived in Forest Gate, East London, near to Stratford. The heavy smoke hanging in the cold morning air was a signal that winter and the long dark nights were on their way.

Many of our neighbours had fought in World War I. Some of them worked in the light industrial units at the end of our road, which included a forge, a sheet-metal works and a panel-beater's workshop that repaired dented cars. They still wore military boots but their army uniform made way for grey three-piece suits, pocket watches and a flat cap. They seemed so old, but were a visible and constant reminder of conflict and loss. They had been through so much: two wars, the Depression, conscription and rationing, and had witnessed some terrible things.

The grey suit was also worn by the postman, the bus conductor and the Tube-train driver. It was a drab symbol of authority that marked a man as having a higher status than those skilled or semi-skilled manual workers who wore overalls. Even so, the grey suit was a world away from the bowler hat, morning dress and rolled umbrellas of the city worker.

As a boy I learned about what men did by their clothes. I knew my father was a manager for example, because he wore a shirt and tie and worked in an office alongside a workshop. I remember one day my father showing me the badges and buttons that were once attached to his army uniform, and I knew these shiny adornments signified bravery, courage and authority that would only be known by some men.

England was limping along on a three-day week under Conservative Prime Minister Edward Heath. The shorter working hours were intended to save electricity in the wake of industrial action by miners, and the television stations even stopped broadcasting at 10.30pm. Central heating was a luxury and many of London's houses were heated by coal or gas fires; some were heated by electric or portable paraffin heaters which could be lethal, and was the cause of many house fires. We had no central heating in our house until 1973. My mother would get up at 7am, around the time my father left for work. She'd light the gas fire in the living room, stand in front of it and smoke a cigarette in her woolly dressing gown.

Everyone I knew worked. My father made weighing machines, joining his company as an apprentice and became a senior manager. He was in charge of engineers all over England, and I was often woken by the phone ringing in our house with an engineer calling about a breakdown at a factory in Manchester, Birmingham or Bristol. They were all skilled workers: mechanics, fitters and scale-makers, and it felt to me as if the world was dominated by well-disciplined working men.

When I started school my mother went to work part-time for my father's company as a bookkeeper in the offices above the workshops. She was quite independent and had her own car – a Ford Popular, which she drove to work. But in the 1970s, there were no women engineers or scale makers; they just worked 'upstairs', in the clean, wood-panelled offices smelling of carbon paper and floor polish.

Along with the industrial units at the end of our road there were also railway arches and yards containing small workshops, including a wood-turner's and a grain store. During the school holidays the arches became a playground. My best friend, Leroy, and I knew all the men who worked there, and watched what they did as we darted from arch to arch. There was Charlie with a bulbous nose, who drove a beautiful white Ford Granada, a model clearly aimed at executives. He sprayed wooden furniture with a sickly, sweet-smelling varnish. Leroy and I made him tea in the afternoon and he'd give us change to buy a Mars bar each for ourselves, in return.

There was Rex, who repaired crashed cars and let us play in those waiting for collection. He told us how he hated his wife and swore as he bent over a Ford Escort to winch out the engine. He always wore a black, woolly hat and was covered in thick black grease, like an industrial comfort blanket protecting him from the world outside – and probably his wife.

At lunchtime we went to the corner café and ate sausages, beans and chips for 24p alongside the men in grey suits, overalls and caps sitting at communal tables. They shared a *Daily Mirror* newspaper, and we played the pinball machine and bagatelle as we waited for our lunch.

Leroy and I were the same age and went to the same school. His parents had emigrated from Jamaica and were proud of their house, with its protective plastic on the furniture and upright piano. We collected die-cast metal Matchbox cars and Action Men in uniform, and would play with them for hours during the holidays on the wall in the front garden that separated my parents' house, where I'd been born, from those of our neighbours. We had enough cars and trucks to fill a large wooden crate. including several fire engines. We rode our Chopper bikes around the block – turning in front of the arches as we acted out our own conflicts with loud banging cap guns and replica rifles. We pretended to kill and be killed, to be the victim and the hero. We had freedom, and the time to learn from the working men. I admired their self-discipline; they made things, looked after their gardens, could paint and decorate their houses.

When I was 10, I was allowed my first pair of boots, and as I slid into the tan Doc Martins, just about ankle high, I took a step closer to manhood. They made me feel tough, and I proudly laced them up imagining myself as a worker. I didn't know anything about university, or who went there, but I knew my future would involve 'doing' things, like a craftsman and working in the services also appealed to me.

My father was a National Serviceman in the 1950s, so was his brother, and my mother's father fought in both world wars. My mother's brother, Uncle Eric, was a merchant seaman who never realised his dream of being a fireman.

It was the time of the Cold War, with a constant threat from the USSR and nuclear Armageddon. The threat of Irish nationalist terrorism in London, was right on my doorstep. I grew up in the hangover from World War II that lasted decades. And I grew up alongside the old men in boots and grey suits: the workers who lost their fathers, their friends and their brothers. An entire generation of women without husbands thanks to the Great War. Every year I watched the Royal British Legion service of remembrance on the television broadcast by the BBC, with my parents and brother in the tiny front room of the terraced house where I was born. The service was always at the Royal Albert Hall and as the poppies fell from high inside its domed roof, I listened carefully for the solemn words:

'When you go home, tell them of us and say, "for your tomorrow, we gave our today."' John Maxwell Edmonds' epitaph was welded to my consciousness, a yearly reminder that I should be grateful for my freedom; and should learn respect, discipline and that one day, I too, would be a worker, and a man. Then followed Laurence Binyon's moving ode at the climax of the service:

'Age shall not weary them, nor the years condemn; at the going down of the sun, and in the morning, we will remember them.'

My father was born in 1937, two years before my mother, their early years marked by a country suffering the hardship of war, and the depression and the austerity that followed it. I was reminded constantly, as I grew up, what it meant to serve your country.

When I was a teenager, I made bonfires in the garden. It was early in the new year and the easiest way of disposing of boxes, wrapping paper and leftover Christmas packaging was to burn the lot, a task my parents trusted me with. I felt good about being given the responsibility. I dug a small pit in the earth on a bare patch next to my father's clipped-for-winter roses. I stood there, alone after school, hoping the fire would burn forever and the pile of rubbish wouldn't run out.

The thick cardboard charred, then split. The wind carried the glowing flakes into the early evening sky and beyond. The plastic bottles softened and collapsed into a malleable lump, then set hard again, the orange flames mesmerising me. It was warm, I was content. I'd go in for tea smelling of smoke, with dirt and ash on my boots, having had a taste of being a man.

I understood that some people were afraid of fire because it was dangerous and could kill, spreading out of control, consuming everything in its path. I experienced this as a young child when, during the 1977 firemen's strike, two children from my school died in a house fire. Many years later, I heard from firemen I knew that crews from Leytonstone turned out, breaking their own picket line to try to save the children.

I discovered a respect for the simple chemical reaction, where oxygen, fuel and heat create combustion known as the triangle of fire. When any side of the figurative triangle is removed, it collapses and the fire is extinguished. So bonfires, barbecues and fireworks all interested me. One day I went to the library and asked the librarian for books about firefighting. She pointed to a shelf packed with hardbacks, and buried in the 'W' section was Fireman! A Personal Account, by Neil Wallington about his time in the London Fire Brigade starting in the 1960s. I took it home and read it all in a couple of days, gripped by Wallington's tales of massive fires in warehouses with burning bales of paper and collapsing walls.

His vivid account of rescues and disasters inspired me and fuelled my interest in becoming a firefighter. With every match I lit, my respect for fire grew. I was drawn to the danger, the colour and the smell without fear of the damage it could cause.

I began to think of joining the fire service as a career and a calling.

When I was 14 I went to an award ceremony with my parents at the City of London Police Station in Wood Street. My older brother, who was a police officer, was being presented with an award for being the top cadet in his class. After the presentation a senior officer spoke to my parents and congratulated my brother. He then turned to me.

'What about you, young man? Are you interested in becoming a police officer?'

'No, I don't think so, sir,' I replied.

'No? What would you like to do then when you leave school?'

'I want to be a fireman, sir.'

'A fireman? That's very interesting. I could never do that. *Oh no*: I couldn't stand all that smoke.' He waved his hand under his nose as if to disperse some imaginary fumes, wincing as though there was a bad smell.

I smiled politely, and thought to myself, *But I could*.

By now there was no other job I wanted to do. I didn't like the idea of joining the army and killing someone. I didn't like the idea of being a policeman and depriving someone of their liberty. I wanted to be a fireman. Everyone loved firemen because they helped people and were heroes. But most of all, I longed to be a man, to wear a uniform and have responsibility.

Later, I wrote to Derbyshire Fire Service which at the time offered a junior fireman scheme, a kind of apprenticeship for 16-year-olds. I couldn't apply because I didn't live in the county. But I hung on to my dream of joining the London Fire Brigade and hoped I'd soon be like my brother and father who both wore uniforms. I, too, would do something out of the ordinary – even if that meant risking my life.

My father had told me stories about his training as a rifle-man, and my mother about how she waited at Waterloo Station to meet him when he came home on leave during his two years in the army. I longed to be a fighter, someone respected for his bravery; someone who fights the enemy, the demon that is fire; someone whose weapons are water and willpower; someone whose job is to save a life, as opposed to take one.

At the start of my second night shift I had 33 hours of operational experience, but had not yet been to a fire.

It was around 9pm when we were called to a fire in a garage in the Forest Gate neighbourhood, about halfway between my house and the fire station. As we pulled up, a derelict building about 30 by 20 feet was alight. I could see the flames from the back of the pump. They rose to about 15 feet and reflected into the pump's cab, lighting up the surrounding street with a bright, orangey tint.

Station Officer Tim Blake, the officer-in-charge, yelled out without even looking around at us, his gaze fixed on the orange flames: 'Inch-and-three-quarter jet and branch! Drop the tank! Get a hydrant in!'

Despite my training I was so excited that I struggled to take in his order, dispatched so quickly. We jumped off the pump, the governor's order lost on me, but it didn't matter, because the other three crew members were unrolling a hose and directing water at the structure in seconds. One length of hose, carried loose in lockers on the side of the machine, was plugged into the pump. Another length of hose was connected to a hydrant, level with the pavement using a standpipe, key and bar.

One of my first responsibilities was to find the nearest hydrant, having looked it up in a directory en route to an incident.

What's your name, mate?' asked a firefighter from a neighbouring station's crew that had turned up to help.

"It's Cliff.'

"Alright, mate?' he asked. I nodded with excitement.

'Knock off the jet!' ordered Station Officer Blake.

'Clifford, get the hose reel on there and start damping down.'

There was a hose reel wound onto a drum on either side of the pumping appliance. They were used on small fires but pumped at extremely high pressure. I wasn't so much fighting a fire but at last I was playing a small part, standing on a charred pile of timber and corrugated metal, cooling the collapsed and tangled remains of the garage.

I shut down the nozzle as the other firefighters pulled the smouldering debris apart. A few minutes later, I opened the nozzle and splashed myself. The water was hot so I closed it again. I felt disorientated and overwhelmed by my new job, excited to be at my first fire, but also confused. I opened the nozzle again and put my hand into the stream. It was still hot. I looked around at Bert, who was operating the pump.

'The water's boiling hot! I don't understand it.'

Bert came over, smiling. 'It's because you've closed the nozzle, but I've been pumping against it at high pressure. The water is circulated round the impeller and with nowhere to go, it causes friction, and the friction heats the water.'

Then Station Officer Blake interrupted us. 'Knock off and make up. Let's get out of here. Bert, book us mobile.'

As we returned to the station, I realised that there was much to learn about my new job: every detail of the equipment, the machines, the procedures and the risks on our ground. Later that night, I was told we'd be going back to the fire to check it hadn't re-ignited.

I made an entry in the watch room logbook before picking up the red phone only used for contacting the control room:

'23:00hrs. To control. Permission requested for pump, station officer in charge, to visit scene of fire at Vansittart Road, E7. Answer: "Yes."'

The fire was out. We returned. Then I recorded the events of the remainder of the shift:

'23:10 hrs. Station secured.

'Saturday 30 November: '06:40 hrs. Called staff.

'07:00 hrs. Station routine commenced.'

I looked at the clock in the watch room. I'd hardly slept, still wasn't hungry, and felt as though I were in a dream or in a film, under the bright lights and high on the moment. The time was 8.59am. I watched as the second hand swept over the six, reached for the lever on the control box that signalled the bells manually, and pressed it downwards with short strokes: six bells and the Red Watch was dismissed.

I'd completed my first tour of duty. I'd taken the first gentle steps towards a lifelong ambition. I had been initiated into an extended family of brothers and began to learn the routine of life on a fire station: repetition, drills and studying.

I'd enjoyed my first fire, but I didn't feel much like a hero.

CHAPTER 2

Required to Engage

It was Friday 13 March 1987, and the old man was sitting in his favourite armchair in the living room of a Victorian terrace in Plaistow, but close to East Ham and Stratford on a typical day, in his ordinary house.

Originally built for young, aspiring, working-class families, there were thousands of these houses in the side roads of Stratford, East Ham and Plaistow. A short hall led to the rear of the house from the front door, with another door on the left to the sitting room, where the original Victorian occupiers spent their evenings reading and entertaining guests. In this sitting room there was a black cylinder of oxygen about 3 feet high. Attached to the top was a regulator, a long clear plastic tube and a face mask with elasticated straps. The living room, which was at the back of the house, was brightly lit that day by a low, early afternoon sun.

At nine that morning, I put on my fire rig for roll call. I'd been at Stratford for just over a year but was still settling into life on the station. I walked from the locker room through the dormitory towards the muster bay but stopped at the end of the dorm. Holding my helmet, wearing the heavy woollen tunic, boots and overtrousers, I suddenly felt a powerful sense of loss. A wave of emotion swept over me, stopping me in my tracks. I sat on the edge of one of the iron beds, my head in my hands. I felt emotionally paralysed, cold and fearful – but of what? I had no idea. One of the Green Watch firefighters who was going off duty walked past. 'Are you OK, Cliff?'

'Yes. Yes, I think so, I just feel a bit... It's OK. I'll be OK.'

'Are you sure, mate? You don't look right.'

'Yes, it's fine—'

The conversation was interrupted by six bells as I struggled to compose myself.

I was confused by what I had felt, but have since formed the opinion that along with other people, I've sometimes experienced a sense of foreboding before a disaster or death.

It happened one night a few years later, when I was asleep in the fold-up bed in the junior officers' room at Ilford. It was quite a small room, with a desk and chair – except the desk was just a modern wood panel fixed to the wall, and a cabinet that contained the bed.

I was dreaming that I was standing at the head of a grave. The earth on top was raised and covered with brightly coloured, fresh flowers. Then I was floating above it, over the headstone. The feeling of detachment, of watching myself, was similar to the floating or ghosting experience I'd had on some of the bigger jobs, or where someone had died. I quickly sat up in bed, half-awake, convinced that I was lying in my own coffin. I thought the dream was a warning about my own death, and I'd been looking at my grave.

The next day, I was at home after the night shift, feeling anxious, so I phoned my friend Kay in Plymouth, who told me her mother had died. I had spent a lot of time in Devon learning to scuba dive in 1987, and became very close to Mrs Snowdon, who was like a surrogate grandmother to me. I even called her grandma – as did everyone who got to know her. She was well-to-do, and lived in an old vicarage on the edge of the River Tamar – a section known as the Hamoaze

- Grandma knew so many people, it was impossible for Kay to tell everyone in time about the funeral. Even though I'd had that dream after she died and was buried, I was sure that it was a warning to those on earth, and believe it's the point when the deceased lets go of the here and now.

Just after lunch we were called to a house fire at 79 Rutland Road. I was riding the pump with two firefighters, Kevin and Roger, and Tom Harries, who'd taken over as the officer-in-charge of the Red Watch a few months before. Lean and wiry, he ran a tight ship and took no nonsense from us. I respected his authority. We were the first machine to reach the fire. No one was rigged in breathing apparatus as the call was on the edge of East Ham's ground, but we'd got there first. As we arrived we could see smoke coming up over the back of the house. There was a neighbour standing at the front door.

'There's someone in there.'

'Roger: make pumps four! Persons reported!' yelled Tom, giving the order to request the number of engines to be made up to four.

'OK, guv!'

'Where the fuck are East Ham? It's their fucking ground!' shouted Tom. 'Get the reel in there, Kev!'

The entrance to the house was narrow so we entered in single file. Tom, and Kev pushed-on without breathing apparatus to the back room while I followed behind. The fire, which was contained in the back room, was burning at an unusually low level, the tip of the flames about halfway up the wall. Kev pulled back the lever on the hose reel and a blanket of spray forced back the smoke and gradually cleared the view. The three of us inched forwards. I was still at the back, dwarfed by Kev's giant frame.

'We've got a body – get the Respirex!' shouted Tom.

'Alright, guv. What we got?' came a voice from East Ham's officer-in-charge whose machine had just arrived.

'Persons reported. I've made pumps four. Get the resuscitator.'

I moved level with Tom and Kev, and was jostled from behind as the crew from East Ham entered the hall. I could hear the sirens as more machines approached the side road, dispatched on the make pumps four call.

The three of us spread out in a line, a few feet from the fire in the living room. There was a man sitting in a sixties-style armchair with flat wooden arms, a thick vinyl padded seat, sloping back and wooden legs. His eyes were wide open, and there was saliva running from his mouth to his chin. His trousers were burnt from the hem to the knee like charred old rags and the skin and flesh on his lower legs had peeled away. The seat of the armchair was smouldering, but there was very little fire damage above the man's waist.

The fire had burned its way downwards with such intensity that it stripped the man's clothing, skin and flesh. It burned a jagged hole around his feet, which had been bare, and downwards through the floorboards exposing the joists and dark void below; the rest of the living room was untouched.

Everything went into slow motion as I focused on the man's eyes. It felt as if I'd left the ordinary world that Friday afternoon and had been thrust into a bizarre film scene. He looked like a charcoal scarecrow with straw protruding from the splits in his clothing. I could see the flesh beneath his sticky, red skin, his shins burnt to the bone. He sat as if he was waiting for the racing to come on the radio, his face expressionless.

'Get the fucking Respirex,' shouted Tom, convinced the

man could be saved. His order wasn't to anyone in particular, but instead of our own resuscitator, one of the East Ham fire-fighters grabbed the large black cylinder from the sitting room.

'Here guv, take this!' He passed it to me, and I passed it to Tom.

'What? What the fuck is this? He must have a problem with his fucking lungs!' shouted Tom, growing more irate by the minute. I watched as Tom and Kev, with their decades of experience, pulled the old man, who was bony and frail, from the chair. They laid him out on the floor close to the living room door as Tom secured the face mask and Kev leaned over and started compressing the man's chest in the hope of starting his heart. There was a loud snap as one of the old man's ribs gave way – the once-heard-never-forgotten sound of a fracturing human bone. Nothing could be done for him.

'OK, leave it there,' said Tom. 'The police and fire investigation team will be here soon. Clifford, make up the hose reel. Roger, send an amended "stop" from me: at 79 Rutland Road – one person found on ground floor, apparently dead.'

'OK, guv,' Roger replied.

I dragged the reel back to the pump and wound it onto the drum. I walked into the front garden and saw a woman walking towards the house. She was wearing smart trousers and sunglasses pushed up into her curly dark hair.

'Excuse me – my dad lives here. Where is dad? Where is he?' she asked, looking around me towards the front door. I was completely lost for words.

Oh fuck, I can't tell her that her father is dead on the floor in the back room, I thought. *How do I tell her? Surely the governor will do it?*

The situation got worse when a photographer from a local paper arrived. He worked for the *Stratford and Newham Express*, and was known for intercepting radio messages from the police and the fire service on a scanner.

'Alright, Graham. Back on the other side of the road,' I said, sounding more confident than I felt.

'What is it? What you got? I hear it's a four-pumper? Fatal, is it?' He fumbled to get his camera up to his eye, oblivious to the daughter standing next to me.

'Come on, you know how it is. Get over the road, Graham.'

The woman went quiet as shock kicked in. All I could think of was the scarecrow image of her father, sitting in the chair.

Tom Harries walked out of the house. The police arrived and she was taken to a neighbour's.

The rest of that day is blank.

My first fire death was a significant milestone. I realised that death can strike anyone, at any time, and a firefighter is often surprised when an innocuous incident in the middle of the day turns out to be fatal. In the days that followed I tried to understand why I'd felt so unsettled at the start of the shift. Was it warning of what was about to happen? Even today, if I'm involved in a big disaster in my job as a journalist I'll often look back with the benefit of hindsight and say I'd felt uneasy in the hours or days leading up to it. But as a firefighter, there was always the hope that something would happen – that was part of the addiction, the almost dirty secret of willing it to.

For a few days afterwards, I felt subdued, struggling to come to terms with the concept of someone living for so long, surviving so much, only for his last moments to be spent with a group of strangers as his body filled with toxic gas and his legs burned.

Station Officer Harries took notes at the scene and the fire-investigation team tested the area around where the fire started with a device that recorded the presence of petrol.

No trace was found. The fire had burned in an uncharacteristic fashion: downwards. The back room was well ventilated so the fire hadn't spread up the walls. The police interviewed the neighbours and the man's daughter, and a few days after the fire an inquest was opened at Poplar Coroners' Court.

It was impossible to know precisely what he'd gone through in his final moments. The subsequent joint police and fire investigation concluded that he had lit a cigarette while sitting in his armchair. He suffered from emphysema, a progressive lung disease that lessened his chances of surviving the toxic fumes. He'd either fallen asleep in the chair, dropping the cigarette that started the fire and was overcome by carbon monoxide. Or he'd dropped the cigarette while he was awake, but was unable to move because of his weakened lungs. To die upright in his chair, with his arms at his side, suggested he had made no attempt to escape but was disorientated and unconscious within a few minutes of ignition. He was unaware of the intensity of the heat building up around his feet, or of the sticky burning foam from the base of the chair dropping onto the carpet. For a fire to destroy the bones, the temperature has to reach the region of 700–900°C: the temperature at which cremation begins to destroy a body.

I had dealt with my first fire death, and was relieved – my stock rose in value, as now I was a real firefighter in the eyes of the Red Watch. During my first year at Stratford I had worn breathing apparatus, been part of the first crew to enter a building on fire, been exposed to chemical incidents and removed my first body from a road traffic accident. I could now add this to my roll call of experiences. On reflection I understand that the sense of detachment I'd felt at seeing my first dead body protected me from the horror I'd witnessed.

Being part of a team, with all of us wearing the same uniform, also provided a degree of psychological protection. I also had an overwhelming sense of relief from having made it through the experience. I was settling into the routine of being a firefighter, and felt pleased at having experienced my first fatality, as opposed to what might have seemed more natural: being horrified.

After six months at Stratford, I was allowed to go on 'out-duties', which meant spending a shift at a neighbouring station to make up their numbers if they were short of firefighters. One of my first out-duties was a busy night shift at Walthamstow. We were sent to stand by at Tottenham for a couple of hours while its crews put out a fire. We had a fire in a flat off Blackhorse Road, and such was my eagerness that I opened the nozzle of the hose reel in the hall, directly behind the crew, causing a fair bit of water damage and showering the two firefighters in front of me.

Then in the early hours of the morning, we were called to a road traffic accident in Forest Road, which spread out across four lanes. A red Volkswagen Scirocco sports car had spun out of control and mounted the railings on the pavement, which buckled, forming a ramp. The force of the collision projected the car so that it was perched on top of the railings, its two nearside wheels off the ground. This was my first road traffic accident.

When we reached the scene, I got stuck in without really knowing what to do. I watched as the roof of the car was cut off in seconds and an unconscious man lifted onto an ambulance stretcher. He was covered by a red blanket with the texture of waffles.

The next day, I felt frustrated. Was he dead, badly injured, or did he recover? Not knowing troubled me. I felt detached as the event unfolded, but troubled by it afterwards. It sometimes felt macabre to look forward to the next working job, but my addiction to the dramas being played out in front of me was growing. It became a pattern. I'd feel removed during a job, as if I were in a dream, and then the severity and complexity of events would sink in much later, often when I was on my own at home, when I would try to rationalise the horror I'd witnessed.

On an earlier occasion, we were called to a person threatening to jump from a high-rise block in Plaistow. Inexperienced in dealing with this sort of emergency, I felt uneasy as we took the lift to the top of the building. I was squashed between two large police officers from the traffic division, one holding a large radio with a foot-long whip aerial. They were laughing as the lift slowly crept up the block. All I could think about was how we had to get there before the man jumped.

'Er, what do we do if we, if we're... I mean we don't want him to jump. We have to get up there quickly,' I said, my voice quivering and sounding every bit the new boy.

'Listen, son,' replied one of the officers, 'If he's still hanging on when we get there...' He flicked the radio level with my eye-line causing the aerial to crack in the air. 'If he's hanging on, I'll whack him on the head with my radio, you see? That'll make the fucker jump!'

I was alarmed. A man's life was hanging in the balance and the police were laughing. I couldn't understand how anyone could become so detached or feel such a lack of compassion. Inside the closed ranks of the police, traffic officers are known as 'rats', and it's not a term of endearment. But their attitude was a result of having seen too much death on the roads. The traffic division probably witnessed the most gruesome injuries and deaths in collisions: heads snapped off at neck flexor joints, eyeballs ejected from their sockets and entire families obliterated by 'one for the road'.

When we reached the 19th floor, the man had been talked around and pulled in from the balcony by another police-man, who had reached the landing before us. I was relieved. I was horrified by the possibility of seeing someone take their own life.

After a year of fighting fires, I realised that my addiction had an inevitable consequence: the come-down or the hango-ver. I was working a 48-hour tour of duty. I slept on the night shift, but also at home for a few hours between nights, and after each tour finished. Then I had four days off. For exam-ple, finishing on a Monday morning meant I'd be back at work for a day shift on Friday then work over the weekend. The cycle moved forward a day each week, so I had lots of time off and was often bored. I thought about leaving home, but a booming property market meant that even a £27,000 studio flat in Forest Gate was out of my range. The economy thrived and a young, upwardly mobile social group emerged that I was not a part of.

But I wasn't doing badly. I was living at home, with a disposable income and a busy social life with my watch-mates and other friends. Someone was always around during the day. We'd meet at the Red Lion pub in Leytonstone in the afternoon and drink for a couple of hours, or play snooker at a club in Wanstead, to fill the time between afternoon and evening. Then we'd go out, every night of the week – except Monday.

I longed for the moment when, standing in a nightclub, I'd be asked by a girl, 'What do you do, then?'

A cheesy smile would stretch across my face as I replied,

'I'm a fireman.'

'Wow, you're brave! Will you give me a fireman's lift?'

'I will if you have a slow dance with me.' I felt a sense of power and played up to the idea of myself as the teen hero.

I started training at a bodybuilders' gym in Leytonstone High Road. It was a bit of a dump, but it gave me something to do during the day. I bench-pressed my way through the afternoon three times a week and put on a stone in muscle. But despite the flirtations, the training, the money and the nightclubs, all I wanted was the start of the next shift and the sound of ringing bells.

Station life gradually became familiar, and my confidence grew with every shout. I had so much energy and enthusiasm. As I settled into my new career, I began to separate my life into three compartments: disaster, action and addiction – the lure of the next working job.

I slept on the iron bed at night in the dormitory and in the watch room when I was a duty man, always keeping on my T-shirt and socks so I could get rigged more quickly. I was much younger than the rest of the Red Watch, the majority of whom were in their 30s and 40s. They were known as '20 year men' – an acknowledgement of the time they had survived fighting fires.

A watch is structured along tribal lines, with its officers and elders the 'old hands' at the top end of the hierarchy right down to its newer firefighters; the junior buck, the most recent watch member to be posted from training school, is at the bottom of the chain. At Stratford, the Red Watch were all senior firefighters, some of whom had served in the smaller borough brigades like West Ham and East Ham, which existed as autonomous bodies until they were brought into an expanded London Fire Brigade controlled by the Greater

London Council – created in 1965. These firefighters were respected due to their long service, but in the modern brigade, such watch members were also rewarded with more holiday entitlement and higher pay in recognition of 'long service'.

The mess was the heart of a fire station and firefighters gathered there for a cup of tea and a chat at the beginning of every shift. It was the ideal place for stories about big fires or disasters to be told and retold – handed down from one firefighter to the next. Experience was also passed on from the senior watch members to the newest recruit in the form of testing and cleaning equipment, which helped the probationer gain confidence and skills to use the equipment under more stressful conditions.

There were no Blitz firefighters at Stratford as it was now so long after the end of World War II, so I missed out on the stories about how London was so badly bombed and the giant blazes it caused. But in the mid-80s, the brigade was still a 'closed shop', which meant all firefighters – including me – had to be members of the Fire Brigades Union. So many of the stories I heard were about how watches were split during the national strike that started November 1977 and created great tension when some firemen crossed the picket lines and worked in the dispute, which ran until January 1978. Shared union membership with its solidarity knitted the watches even tighter together.

The Moorgate Tube train crash in the City of London, which killed 43 people in 1975, also became part of the brigade's folklore; a firefighter who had attended Moorgate and served through the strike commanded the most respect. Such incidents were like badges of honour that set these firefighters apart. Watches functioned as tribes, even as families with their unique heritage and bond, and I was made to feel that I was following in the footsteps of the great.

Before night shifts some of the watch went to the Three Pigeons pub across the road. I went into the locker room before one shift and knew I was gradually earning my spurs on the watch when I was greeted by 'It's Cliff!' It reinforced my sense of becoming part of the team. The banter followed a similar format, usually led by Roger Laker, one of the older men on the watch who I respected most. I felt he was looking over my shoulder and making sure I was OK.

Roger and Bert Lewinton always went to the pub. If they were driving they'd only drink two pints, usually bitter. They were both old enough to be my father and helped me settle into the watch. There was always excitement at the start of a night shift.

'It's going to be the big one tonight, Cliff,' Roger always said.

'A chance to make a name for yourself,' added Bert.

Then Danny Shore joined the banter. 'What, another name? As well as all the others, like "you little shit"?' Everyone laughed.

I took it in my stride and remembered the words of my instructor at training school: 'If you can't take a joke, you shouldn't have joined the job.'

I was no longer watching the men at work, but taking my place alongside them. Every one of them addicted, they'd all served 'in the smoke' of busy central London stations. They all loved fighting fires. On one day shift, Bert turned up with his brigade shirt covered in blood after he stopped to help a dying man knocked off his motorbike. Bert had taken his shirt off to stem the bleeding. Their hearts were full of compassion and love.

I loved the attention being a firefighter brought me – and the way it could increase my status at the station. One day, a girl called Kerry, who had gone to my school, started appearing in a club I went to on a Friday night. She lived behind Leytonstone fire station and decided she wanted to date a fireman. I was almost 20, and the thought of going out with a 16-year-old didn't appeal.

She soon became part of my social network. One night shift, I was riding the pump with another firefighter, Danny Shore. We were sent to stand by at Leytonstone fire station and when their pump returned, Danny asked the governor if we could take a ride up the high road so he could go to a cash machine. We stopped outside a bank, and Danny jumped out of the cab and got his cash. When the door opened again I heard him laughing.

'You want to see Cliffy?' he said to someone on the pavement. 'Oi! Cliffy, you little shit: look who's here to see you, mate.'

'What are talking about?'

'Look – there's someone to see you.' He laughed.

'Fuck off.'

Then I heard him say, 'Look, there he is,' as he lifted a girl off the pavement so she was level with me in the cab.

There was more giggling. 'Hello, Cliff,' said Kerry as she peered into the back of the cab at me. 'Just someone who wants to say hello,' said Danny.

I was super-cool, my right boot pressed up on the bulkhead dividing front and rear cab as I looked at her.

'Alright, darling. How are you?'

'Ah, look at you in your uniform. Are you out on Saturday?' Kerry asked.

'Yeah, always babe.'

'Alright, see you then.'

Danny couldn't wait to tell the rest of the watch when we got back to Stratford. Learning to keep my cool was an essential part of the job, but my status increased for having a young secret admirer. I was revelling in it, and the older men were jealous at the attention I got.

I had a regular girlfriend, Colette, at the time. We'd met in a club in 1984 when I was in the second year of my engineering apprenticeship, having left school at 16. Five years older than I was, she was training to be a nurse. She was from County Offaly in Ireland (she took me to visit her family over there) and spoke with a calming and smooth, sultry accent. We had a lot in common, and when I was posted to Stratford she talked to me about 'surviving' night shifts and dealing with the stress of saving other people's lives, and what happened when it wasn't possible. She witnessed death every day – but in a hospital environment. Colette and I grew to understand each other's worlds. We were serious, and I thought I'd marry her by the time I was 25 and have children. But once I joined the fire service I was so pre-occupied by my work that I could never fully commit.

I'd known I wanted to be a firefighter since the age of 14, and would often wonder if it was possible to train someone to cope with the death of another. I remember talking to my parents about it once while out in the car. I was sitting in the back, my mother in the front next to my father. 'I'm going to apply to join the brigade,' I announced. I'd been to several fire station open days, and had been adopted by a watch at Homerton, who allowed me to visit during the school holidays to find out as much as I could about the job.

'Well, that's great, but do you think you could cope with

seeing a dead body?' my father asked.

'Yes, of course,' I said confidently, although I had no idea how I'd cope with death. I knew I had to grow physically stronger. I'd started playing rugby in an effort to toughen up – and harden myself emotionally. I was far from indestructible but one day, at the age of 15, my courage was tested.

It was mid-afternoon and I was getting off a bus with my first serious girlfriend, Elaine, as it pulled into a stop at a lay-by on a busy dual carriageway outside the Tube station in Wanstead. As we stepped down onto the pavement and the doors closed, I heard a loud sucking noise behind me. I looked around to see an elderly lady in a beige coat fall onto the road and then under the bus. Her legs were crushed by the giant rear wheels as the bus drove off, the bus driver oblivious to what had just happened. As the bus accelerated, she was ejected with considerable force. Elaine and I doubled back. 'Run to the Underground and phone an ambulance,' I said.

I ran after the bus as the driver sped up, hoping to catch him at the next stop. But it soon disappeared out of view. If I kept running, I'd be further away from Elaine, so I turned around and ran back. The woman was lying in a lake of blood, which was running into the drains. I looked at her sur-rounded by her belongings; both her smart brown shoes had been fired off by the force of the tyres. So bad were her inju-ries, she almost didn't look human.

'Have you called the ambulance?' I asked Elaine.

'Yes, and they're sending the police too.'

'The poor woman. She looks so badly hurt.'

I knew a little bit of first aid, but had no idea where to start.

'It's OK,' said Elaine. 'The ambulance is on its way.' A crowd of passengers from the Tube station has begun to gather around the woman.

'It's going to be OK. We saw what happened and we've called an ambulance,' I told them.

A police car pulled-up, followed by an ambulance. We spoke to the officer, who told us the woman's injuries looked life-threatening. I wished I could have done more to help, but she was in a critical condition, and the policeman praised us for our efforts.

'Don't worry; you did all the right things. We'll send a car to the terminus and speak to the driver.'

'Can you all get back!' yelled the ambulance man at the onlookers. 'Just go away – this is going to be very unpleasant, and we need to move her.' Elaine and I stayed with the constable. We were close to the victim as she was lifted onto a stretcher, blood pouring from her tangled legs and hanging torn muscle.

The police officer told Elaine and me to make a note of everything we saw, explaining that if the lady died there'd be an inquest and as the first people on the scene to have helped her, we would be called as witnesses. We went to a café and made some notes on the back of an order pad. A couple of days later the officer came to my house and took a statement. He explained that it looked as though the woman's coat had got caught in the doors as she was getting off the bus. She was trapped, and as she stepped down in panic, forcing herself free, she lost her balance and fell under the wheels.

The last I heard from the police was that she was in an intensive-care unit. I was never asked to attend an inquest, so I assumed she lived but I also knew she'd have been left badly disabled by such a terrible accident. I felt proud that I'd helped and not just walked away. I had coped with a traumatic event, and believed that if I could handle that, I could handle anything.

In 1985, I was working as an apprentice engineer, having left school two years before. I hadn't been very academic and left school with poor qualifications. I hated my job, but was still determined to join the fire service and knew that having a trade with practical skills would help me. Leaving home at 5.30am every morning and travelling on three buses was hard work, and a world away from the freedom, fun and adventures that came with the school holidays: the soldiers, the model cars and the arches. One morning, I noticed an advert for firefighters to join the London Fire Brigade in the *Daily Mirror*. It was a big recruitment drive, so I decided to apply.

I was called up to the Methodist Central Hall in Westminster that spring to take the aptitude test. On arrival I was ushered into the entrance to the hall, my chest measured and my height recorded. 'Thompson? Stop there! Stand against the wall,' came the order from a Station Officer in a white shirt. 'Five feet eight inches!' he shouted to an assistant who wrote it down on a clipboard. 'I'm going to put this tape-measure around your chest, OK? That's 37 inches.' The detail was recorded. 'OK expand your chest: that's 39 inches. You're OK, son. Over there and find yourself a desk for the test.'

The first hurdle to achieve my dream had been cleared. The minimum requirements were a 36-inch chest that could expand by two inches, and a height of five-feet six-inches.

In May I had an interview and a medical, after which I received a letter:

24 June 1985

Dear Sir,

I hereby offer you appointment from Monday, 8 July 1985, in the service of the Greater London Council as a fireman in the London Fire

Brigade on terms under which you would be required to engage in firefighting.

If you wish to accept this appointment you are asked to report on the above date in the first instance to:

The London Fire Brigade Training Centre

94 Southwark Bridge Road, SE1

For recruit training and must book into the Training Centre Office not later than 8.30am on the date of your appointment. The training course will last approximately 14 weeks... your starting salary will be £8,247 a year.

It was signed on behalf of the chief staff officer, Personnel and Administration Branch, and accompanied by a thick pile of papers including a contract and a separate letter from the chief medical officer advising me to have a tetanus injection to 'protect me from lockjaw'. I liked the idea of being 'required to engage in firefighting.' It sounded very grown up.

My training would be the first step in protection from all sorts of hazards: nuclear, biological, radioactive, fire, heat, chemical, heat exhaustion and shock. But there were some things from which protection was impossible.

We were well into our training at Southwark when I learned that teamwork and discipline were important factors in handling the rigours of firefighting. I was fortunate that out of a squad of 12 recruits, nine were ex-servicemen, including a Royal Marine who'd not long returned from the Falklands War. They were extremely disciplined and I respected the fact that I was training with men, some twice my age, who had killed other men. Although not a serviceman, I was an Air Cadet, so I had plenty of experience of discipline and knew how to fire several types of small-bore rifles.

One afternoon, we were sitting in a small classroom at the training centre when our instructor, Station Officer Samuels, brought a box of pictures for us to look at. A fiery Welshman on a permanent short fuse, he'd get so angry with us if we made mistakes that he'd foamed at the mouth. But on this day he remained calm. He opened the box and passed around the pictures. 'Look here – you're going to see some pictures of stiffs. These are some of the jobs we go to.'

The brigade photographer turned out to every fatal fire and photographed dead bodies in situ. Firefighters are trained not to disturb a body from which life has obviously gone and are often key witnesses, giving evidence in coroners' hearings and criminal proceedings.

We were sitting in rows on benches along the edges of the room, six on each side, our backs to each other. The prints were large and in colour. The room fell silent as the photos were passed from man to man. My muscles tensed in antici-pation. I had never seen a stiff. I concentrated hard as I was handed a large print first of a body in a house fire, then one of a man trapped in a car ramp, his intestines protruding from his bottom like a string of sausages. There was another of a man impaled on some railings. Station Officer Samuels told us the story that accompanied the print: the man had jumped from a second-floor window, about 40 feet up, after being caught by the husband of a woman he was thought to have been having an affair with. He had launched himself away from the building in an attempt to clear the railings at street level, but had failed. He was impaled on an iron spike through the nape of his neck; the point protruded though his throat. As I looked at the photo, I could see the man's face and his partially dressed body. His head was tilted skywards like a foul-hooked fish, his feet dangling. Samuels told us fire crews from Euston were called out to cut away the railings. The iron spike was removed, but he was dead.

I was struck by the image because, although dead, he still *look*ed like a man. His features were clear. Some of the squad looked to see how I reacted. I kept calm, and all 12 of us were quiet with professional respect. I looked at Pete, the erstwhile Royal Marine, knowing he'd seen much worse, and wondered how he felt about *taking* a life. We left the class that day in a quiet, sober mood. There was nothing to boast about from this experience. It was part of our initiation into a world of tragedy, with far worse to come.

Dead bodies in fires often don't look human such is the distortion. Sometimes the fire is so intense that bodies are reduced to broken parts and ash. The conditions in a fire have a dramatic effect on its victims. The intense heat can contract muscles and bend and twist limbs. Sometimes victims are discovered in a pugilistic stance – on their knees, doubled over, giving the appearance of praying. Sometimes the arms are raised as if protecting the face. Burns to the lining of the throat from inhaled super-heated gases force the tongue to swell and protrude. Soot stuck to the larynx and trachea indicates to the fire investigator whether or not the person was alive when the fire started. Limbs can be easily torn off if an attempt is made to rescue a body.

The amount of ventilation and the intensity of the heat can affect how a body burns. Some are only scorched, so the victim's clothing and hair reveal much about them. They can even be discovered dead in a room adjacent to where the fire started, poisoned by carbon monoxide. Sometimes they are caked in a thick layer of greasy soot, like tragic rag dolls with blackened skin exposing raw flesh deep into the muscle.

My attitude to the horrors I would see during my time in the fire service was shaped very much from a position of acceptance: the acceptance that terrible things do happen to people. The horrific pictures we were shown at training school brought home the reality of the disastrous situations some people got into, and gave us a taste of what we could expect in our future careers. Accepting the truth of what can, and does happen is, I believe, essential when dealing with a fatality at such close proximity. I put it all down to experience, and the more I gained, the more immunised I felt against the general unpleasantness. The week-long St John Ambulance first aid course also helped in training us to deal with many life-threatening scenarios. But however immunised I might have felt against the horrors of what I saw and dealt with, the real impact was burying itself under the surface while I looked and felt, as if I was coping.

CHAPTER 3

Body 115

Imagine a fire so deadly that your face is burnt away and your identity erased. A subterranean hell that is hot, dark, and inescapable. Now imagine dying and your family not even knowing about it. It's difficult to comprehend.

In East Finchley Cemetery, North London, there was a tombstone above a grave, a simple memorial to an 'unknown man'. For 16 years his identity was a mystery. He puzzled fire investigators and forensic scientists; they had a body but no name, no next-of-kin, and no possible way of identifying him. He was buried hundreds of miles from his hometown, with a pauper's funeral service, paid for by the local authority.

London's streets are littered with 'unknown' men and women. In 2015, St Mungo's, the charity for homeless people, stated there were around 7000 rough sleepers on the streets of the capital, and thousands more in hostels and temporary accommodation. People on the streets drop out of the system, disappear from records, their anonymous lives often terminated early by ill-health.

The Finchley grave's occupant became a career-long obsession for Ian Wilkinson, who was an inspector with the British Transport Police. He was given the task of investigating the fire in which the unknown man had died, his family unaware of his demise. His simple coffin was placed on top of that of another man, Ralph Humberstone, who had perished in the same fire. Both men were buried on 11 November 1988. The unknown man was called Body 115.

It was November 1987. We were on Leytonstone's ground, pumping out a flooded basement. Station Officer Tom Harries sent a radio message requesting the damage-control tender from Chingford with a low-level pump. Raw sewage was mixing with water leaking from a burst main and flooding a row of houses. We lifted manhole covers in the street to try to find the source of the leak. It was a freezing dark evening, just after the start of our night shift, and the tail-end of the evening rush hour. It was also a frustrating job. My fire gear was wet, I'd been up and down the stairs to the basements of three large semi-detached houses. The area was known as Upper Leytonstone because it was considered more well-to-do than the shabbier, surrounding neighbourhood.

Roger Laker was driving the pump that night. He walked over from the machine.

'There's a job going on the Underground, guv – in town,' he said to Tom Harries.

'Wonder what that is,' he replied. I thought it sounded interesting. I was getting fed up: my rubber boots covered in shit, my body aching with the piercing cold and the damp.

'I hope we get out of here soon – I'm starving,' I said, and sighed. When the damage-control tender arrived with the special pump, we left the job to a crew from Leytonstone and returned to Stratford.

Nine miles away Soho's pump, call sign Alpha two-four-two, booked in at King's Cross train station just north of the West End. It was just after 8.20pm. During the two-and-a-half-hour period of the 'evening rush hour', which started at 4.30pm that day, 100,000 people passed through the station.

Soho's pump was joined by machines from Clerkenwell and Manchester Square; the call was actually on Euston fire station's ground, but its crews were dealing with another job. Twelve minutes earlier a passenger travelled up one of the station's escalators. When he got to the top he reported the smell of burning to a London Underground booking clerk in the ticket office.

Another passenger could see a glow underneath 'escalator four', which served the Piccadilly Line; he also saw smoke 'about two-thirds of the way up'. He pressed the emergency stop button and shouted at other passengers not to walk up the now-static escalator. A ticket collector left his position by the exit barrier and went to investigate.

By chance, four officers from the British Transport Police (BTP) were on foot patrol at King's Cross station. Its officers are usually deployed to incidents on the rail network by car or van, or travel on trains and the London Underground. Some train stations have BTP stations or offices attached to them.

Two of the police constables, Terry Bebbington and Kenneth Kerbey, were in an operations room in the Tube station's ticket hall. Their radios didn't work below the surface, and they were part of the BTP's British Rail division rather than the 'L Division', which was responsible for the Underground, and therefore had much less local knowledge and experience of the area.

Watching events develop, Kerbey and Bebbington left the ops room to investigate. PC Bebbington went to escalator four, which led from the Piccadilly line to the ticket hall, to investigate the fire. It was deep below street level, where the five Tube lines converge in a complex jumble of tunnels, shafts and escalators. Seeing what he later described as 'a single flame', PC Bebbington returned to the surface and called his control room, who passed the details to the London Fire Brigade's now centralised Command and Mobilising Centre in Lambeth.

In East London, we returned to Stratford, and our thoughts turned to supper. We were called out soon after the start of the shift and we knew Carol the night cook was preparing lasagne and chips, our last chance to eat on the station until breakfast the next morning.

By 19:37 hours, in King's Cross, 'light smoke' was visible in the station entrance and two minutes later the police started the evacuation of the ticket hall. In charge of Soho's pump was Red Watch Station Officer Colin Townsley. On Clerkenwell's pump, Temporary Sub Officer Bell; Station Officer Osborne was in charge of Manchester Square's pump. At the time the first fire crews arrived, 'not a single drop of water' had been used on the fire by any of the train or Underground station staff beneath the ground.

At 19:44 hours, Station Officer Townsley was now above the escalator in the ticket hall, having returned from the seat of the fire. Sub Officer Bell descended the escalator to prevent passengers from walking towards the burning escalator while Station Officer Townsley ordered Fireman Flanagan to send a radio message: 'Make pumps four. Persons reported.'

Two other British Transport Police officers in the vicinity of the fire when it started were PC Stephen Hanson and PC Patrick Balfe, who were standing on the British Rail mainline station concourse, a short distance from the Tube lines ticket hall.

PC Hanson intercepted PC Bebbington's message to call the fire brigade, and along with Balfe descended into the Tube train ticket hall and ordered Underground staff to leave the area. A fifth police officer, PC Julian Dixon, also arrived in the ticket hall, where he was met by Bebbington, who told him, 'Wait here for the LFB to arrive,' before returning to the fire. Two other 'L Division' officers arrived, who put in a 999 call from the King's Cross operations room requesting that 'Piccadilly and Northern Line trains should not stop at King's Cross.'

Then, at 19:45 hours, beneath escalator four, there was an almighty *whoosh*, a crackling sound of fire, as a jet of high-pressure flames shot up the escalator tunnel, filling it, hitting the ceiling and travelling all the way along to the ticket hall a considerable distance away. Underground staff, passengers who were still piling off Tube trains, and the emergency service crews were subjected to the most feared and devastating firefighting phenomenon: a flashover. The explosive rush of unstoppable flames burning at around 500°C swept away everything in its path, claiming many lives with devastating force in a matter of seconds.

PC Hanson made his way up from the escalator just as the jet of flames reached the ticket hall and swirled towards him. Seriously injured, he managed to escape into Euston Road.

I stood in the watch room at Stratford, leaning against the radiator, comforted by its warmth against my legs. We didn't have a main-channel radio in the watch room, so we listened to messages from the incident on the pump's radio, which was parked in the appliance bay. We turned the volume up, a constant stream of messages echoed around the station as machines and officers booked in at the fire.

At King's Cross, PC Dixon was near the exit on the south side of Euston Road, at street level. He helped PC Hanson into the street, then picked up his radio and called the control room: 'Initiate major incident procedure.'

Those four words are a codified protocol that immediately escalates an incident to the highest-possible level of severity and a pre-determined sequence of events follows. Hospitals across London are put on red alert and clear all non-emergency cases in preparation to receive the most seriously injured. Fire appliances not dealing with emergency calls elsewhere are ordered to return to base. Squadrons of ambulances, fast-response units and paramedics in cars and on motorcycles are pulled into the capital, and local authority emergency planning officers prepare evacuation centres and temporary accommodation for those who might be displaced by the disaster.

Crash teams in accident and emergency units abandon them and drive to the designated command position, while their off-duty colleagues are called in or volunteer to help. In London, what was known at the time as G-Hems – the emergency medical helicopter based during daylight hours at the Royal London Hospital in Whitechapel is deployed, as are the Metropolitan Police's helicopters, with their unique 'India' call-sign, based at Lippitts Hill, deep in Epping Forest, from where they lift to give an overview of the incident.

A police headquarters is (typically) nominated as Gold Command: where the operation will be run from, with senior officers from the three main blue-light emergency services. And in the corridors of government, the prime minister, secretaries of state, ministers and their advisers assemble at COBR – the Cabinet Office Briefing Room, sometimes referred to as COBRA: the UK's emergency response 'bunker' where the committee plans the resources, personnel and equipment that will be needed to respond, including those from emergency services all over the UK under a

scheme called mutual aid. The British Red Cross, The
Salvation Army, St John Ambulance and the military can all
be called on to supply additional personnel and equipment
from anywhere in the UK.

In the watch room, the teleprinter was chattering constantly. Messages from the King's Cross fire were being
relayed to every station in London because of the incident's
severity. At 19:53 hours, in the LFB control room, a control
officer informed London Underground's Headquarters
Controller that there was a 'full fire at King's Cross.' Then, at
20:03, the message 'Make pumps 12. Make ambulances four,'
was sent, transcribed and relayed to every fire station in
London by teleprinter.

Two minutes before, BTP Inspector Ian Wilkinson arrived
at King's Cross on a Piccadilly Line Tube train. Then at
20:16, the London Ambulance Service declared 'Major accident procedure', putting hospitals across the capital on red
alert. University College Hospital (UCH) was the designated
main hospital. St Bartholomew's, known informally as Barts
in the City of London, was the support medical facility. A
press liaison point was set up at UCH in anticipation of a
large media interest. As the severity of the King's Cross fire
became apparent, interest from the international media grew,
aware of the possible consequences of such a terrible fire
beneath the surface on a major transport network.

We stood in small groups, stunned by what we were hearing. I held my breath every time the teleprinter sounded.
Would the tinny message bell be followed by the call-out
bells? I thought we'd get called on, or at the very least moved
to another station to stand by. The anticipation became
unbearable. 'Make pumps 15,' then, 'Make pumps 20.' We
didn't move.

At 20:06, Inspector Wilkinson sent a radio message to the BTP control room, stating that the fire had been extinguished. Seven minutes later, he called up again, telling officers in the Information Room that the fire was 'blazing fiercely'.

Assistant Chief Officer Albert 'Joe' Kennedy was in charge of the LFB's North East Area of London; around 30 stations, he was one of London's most senior fire officers. He took command at King's Cross an hour after the first machines arrived. At 21:11 he gave the order: 'Make pumps 30.' Bringing the total number of frontline firefighters to 150, with about another 50 senior officers, staff officers and specialist crews. Shortly afterwards a total of 14 ambulances were lining the streets around King's Cross.

At Stratford I couldn't believe what I was hearing. A 30-pumper. I'd never heard of a fire so big, and a major incident as well. And still we didn't move. Then Bob came into the watch room. 'I think we've lost someone. There's a rumour. A governor from up west, and lots of people are dying.'

I wasn't mentally equipped to deal with this: a Red Watch officer, dying while we were on-duty. The mood sank at Stratford. A serious fire below ground, passengers dying, one of ours lost.

London Fire Brigade officers at King's Cross were radioed and told to 'call the control room by landline'. I heard that message on the pump's radio, and knew that meant it was extremely serious. Information needed to be conveyed but not picked up on an unencrypted FM channel, which in turn could be heard on some home radios or a scanner.

Stratford was dark, it felt black, as we listened to the horror unfolding. We were just eavesdropping, unable to assist our colleagues or the victims. A 'fire surrounded message' was sent by Assistant Chief Officer Kennedy at 21:48, but it took until 01:46 for the 'stop' to be sent, which concluded the fire-fighting part of a job, although relief crews would be needed for many hours yet, and well into the coming days.

I thought there was no point making up my bed. I was sure we'd go on a relief and although I knew this fire was horrific, I wanted to be there: the action was calling. It felt worse not being there, wondering what was happening, how many had perished. I was at the height of my addiction and this was the biggest job ever, so of course I wanted to be part of it. The *BBC Nine O'Clock News* went on-air and had a live phone interview with a reporter at the fire, although the graphic nature of it was still being handled with extreme caution.

Later that night the full extent of what happened emerged. The statistics were shocking: 30 people died in the King's Cross fire (one later in hospital, bringing the total to 31). We remained in the station all night at Stratford. We weren't called on, and the pump wasn't even sent to stand by at another station, or deployed as a relief. Usually there would be a buzz around the station when a working job was in progress, but with so many deaths, including one of our own, the Red Watch were stunned into silence.

We put the television on in the mess at six in the morning, the entire watch drained with exhaustion, on the come-down from an adrenaline high caused by a job we didn't attend. BBC One's *Breakfast Time* attempted to shed some clarity on the events of the previous night. We saw the first pictures of the fire, including some recorded in the ticket hall. We switched to the other channel ITV's *TV-AM* programme and a reporter commented that, 'Hours after the fire, metal ticket machines in the ticket hall were still too hot to touch.' The pictures showed ceramic tiles stripped from the walls and the ceiling collapsed onto the concourse. The reporter explained that stairways acted as chimneys worsening the flames. Then we saw pictures from much earlier in the fire, with firefighters not wearing breathing apparatus running into one of the long tunnels heavy with smoke. The footage showed crews emerging from the inferno wearing breathing apparatus and collapsing with exhaustion. And then the moving images of bodies shrouded in red ambulance blankets being wheeled away on stretchers.

In the confusion, two men were caught up in the fire. One was thought to be sleeping rough somewhere in the tunnels. The second was homeless man Ralph Humberstone. It was later discovered that Humberstone, originally from Lincolnshire, lived in a flat in Elephant and Castle, south London, and was a casual worker in a restaurant in Waterloo. His body was discovered in a passage leading away from the booking hall, although it was unclear what he was doing at King's Cross. It was assumed that he was caught in the flashover but somehow managed to escape to the passageway.

But nothing was known about the other man, who was so badly burnt he was beyond identification. He was removed to a mortuary and given a new identity, Body 115, the simple detail written on a tag and attached to his body.

The fire also claimed the life of Station Officer Colin Townsley, the governor of Soho Red Watch. His body was found at the foot of the steps leading to the Pancras Road station entrance, his uniform and body later described as 'unburned.' Close to him was the body of Elizabeth Byers, who was severely burned. At the inquiry that followed, Station Officer Townsley's actions were singled out: 'He died a hero's death giving his life in an attempt to save another.'

A week later, we were finishing a night shift with one more to follow. I usually went home, slept and ran some errands, but today the Stratford Red Watch were going to a funeral.

I didn't know Colin Townsley. I couldn't imagine what the past week was like for the Soho Red Watch returning from a fire, riding a crew of four instead of five, his abandoned shoes, his locker full of kit. Colin was the first firefighter to die at a job in my two-and-a-half-year career. Firefighters looked up to the station officer or 'the governor': a figure of authority and respect. He stood out wearing a white shirt, unlike ours, which were blue. It was possible for a recruit to reach the rank of station officer after five years' service. So in theory, a fire-fighter joining the brigade at the age of 18, could become a 'governor' by the age of 23. The station officer was our man-ager but he rode with us to fires. We affectionately called him 'the old man': a term of endearment in respect of his experi-ence. We obeyed his orders without question and he had the power to put us on a charge for our misdemeanours, for which we were punished. But we also drank with him in the pub, a father figure when we had a problem. Day and night, shift-after-shift, watches lived together like families, sharing meals, playing snooker and watching films, side-by-side in a close bond.

By the second half of the 1980s, there were still only a handful of female firefighters (excluding the many control officers). London was among the first brigades to accept women, full time in 1982. About 60 women joined the bri-gade, but nearly a decade later the number had reduced to 50. I didn't know any women firefighters and never worked with any, beyond one or two shifts when a female firefighter was sent to stand by at Stratford.

It took a long time for attitudes to women firefighters to change; after all, it had been a male preserve in an organised brigade for well over a century, despite the fact that many women served in the fire service during World War II. On a practical level, stations had to be adapted to provide female changing rooms, toilets and showers. At present, there are many more female firefighters and officers, with some going on to become chiefs. By 2017 there were 324 women firefighters in London – approximately seven per cent of the operational workforce, the same year Dany Cotton was appointed as the brigade's first commissioner or chief officer.

I spent the previous week feeling helpless and angry: at the years of training and the experience of a colleague, lost forever. Although I'd never been to an incident on Soho's ground or knew any of its Red Watch, we all came together at times of loss to support each other. Deep down we were all the same: the same training, the same union. The Fire Brigades Union then was a closed shop, so everyone had to be a member. It campaigned tirelessly to improve working conditions for firefighters, and there were many changes brought about because of what happened at King's Cross.

On the morning of Friday, 27 November, three days after my 21st birthday, I stood in the locker room at Stratford, shining my shoes with spit and polish until I could see my reflection in them. I put on my smartest dark uniform trousers. Then, instead of the uniform jacket, I put on a heavy tunic, attached a polished webbing axe-belt with a large shining chrome buckle and a cap, its peak pulled down over my eyes. This is what we wore for a guard of honour.

I walked out of the fire station towards Stratford Shopping Centre on my own. London Underground let us travel free that day and I got on a Central Line Tube train making sure no one would catch my eye. Some of the watch travelled together, but I didn't want to talk, and I didn't fancy a pint beforehand. I couldn't stop thinking about what it must have been like at King's Cross the week before, and wanted to go to the funeral alone. Even though a funeral serves as a reunion, or a coming together of those with a common bond, I just wanted to spend the day by myself.

The scene outside King's Cross train station was amazing. There were firefighters from all over Europe, a mass of uniforms. Colin Townsley's family accepted the brigade's offer of a full ceremonial funeral, and today he was going to be treated like a general, with accompanying honours. Each fire station was told exactly where along the route its firefighters would be positioned. At last I was at King's Cross, and the events of that week became even more real. As I came out of the Underground, I saw Deputy Assistant Chief Officer John Taylor, who was one rank below Assistant Chief Officer Kennedy. My right arm flew up in a smart naval salute.

'Firefighter Thompson reporting, sir. Good morning.'

'Hello, Clifford. How are you? Stand easy,' replied Taylor.

'I'm well, sir. It's a shame to see you in such circumstances, though.'

The image of the uniforms, the mass gathering, the shaking of hands, enthusiastic greetings was powerful: so much solidarity at a time of grief. Hundreds of men gathered as if going forward into battle. There was low-key banter in the air: 'Tomo: haven't seen you in ages...', 'Hey, Smudger. How are you, old bastard?', 'Look it's Bunny Warren...'

Cigarettes were rolled, exchanged and discreetly puffed, hip flasks appeared from the under the flanks of one or two tunics. I felt so lost but was surrounded by men, all of whom would stick their necks out for me. I thought of battles and war: the Somme, Dunkirk, Falklands. I thought of lonely men going over the top, the damp the trenches and the rats. I thought of a nation of women left on their own during the Great War, their husbands never returning.

Then I heard a very loud voice above the buzz.

'London Fire Brigade Guard of Honour. Guard of Honour. In three ranks: fall in!' It was Station Officer Watson, a former army man and one of the smartest I'd seen, and an instructor during my training.

We lined up. The entire front of King's Cross station was masked by hundreds of firefighters, and I felt a sense of relief because all I had to do now was exactly what I was told. A sense of pride helped keep my emotions in check.

Colin Townsley's cortege left Soho fire station. His coffin was placed on a platform across the open chassis of a long turntable ladder. When retracted, the large ladders were about 30 feet long, nearer 100 when extended vertically. The coffin, draped in the Union Flag, and the ladders formed the shape of a cross, and the vehicle was driven slowly along a route lined by thousands of people: passers-by, well-wishers and firemen and -women. There were three firefighters standing sentry on either side of the platform of the machine as it crawled through a hushed central London. Unlike our black webbing belts, they wore white, and white gloves. An entire brigade was in mourning.

I was standing on parade, directly outside King's Cross station and could feel the atmosphere fading to quiet; I knew the cortege was approaching. Reporters hurried around the ranks of firefighters as bulky television cameras were lugged into position. The lens-men appeared, eager to capture the moment for the national papers from the best spot, which was opposite us, with the white King's Cross sign on the canopy of the station in the background.

I stood calm, poised, ready for the order.

From my right I could see the turntable ladder easing along Euston Road, its low rumbling engine the only sound audible.

'Guard of honour: atten-*shun*!' screamed the voice of Station Officer Watson. I pushed my arms down until they were rigid, my left foot snapped towards the right and a noise like a thousand cocking-rifles echoed across the chilly air.

The cortege stopped directly in front of me with Colin Townsley's coffin, the ladders covered in flowers. It paused for a minute's silence at the point where, a week earlier, Colin had died. I tilted my head back with pride to honour a lost hero who would never go home again.

The ladders passed and the order was given by the Station Officer Watson to stand easy. My rigid body relaxed, then after a few minutes, the order was given and we fell out.

I walked over to the cordoned-off entrance to the myriad of tunnels. There was a flight of steps from street level down into the Underground ticket hall; it was in front of the entrance to the train station, which was open. I crouched in front of a mass of cards flowers and cuddly toys. As I squatted I felt as though I was being watched. I slipped deep into thought, trying to make sense of this disaster, determined not to break down as a tear rolled down my cheek.

Then I felt a presence. To my left I could hear the whispering of someone praying, but couldn't make sense of it. I felt as though I was being pulled down, but the whispering was holding me, urging me to get up. It was a powerful force as I felt I was slipping, lower, lower. Lower still, as though the hell beneath my feet was beckoning. The fiery place where so many lives were lost and so much pain endured; where souls were stolen without the knowledge of their loved ones.

I looked to my left and there was a woman crouching next

to me, whispering. I didn't know what she was saying but her voice was calming. When I slowly rose to my feet I saw that she was praying. I walked away. I'd seen enough and needed to decompress, but I still didn't feel like drinking with my colleagues, who dispersed to local pubs. I didn't want to meet up with the rest of my watch mates from Stratford. I took the Tube back to east London and reported at six that night for the second night shift that would take me around to the end of the tour of duty.

The day after the funeral, *Today* newspaper published a picture of a white floral tribute – a station officer's helmet. Behind it, more flowers, also in white that simply spelled 'guv'.

Colin Townsley's widow, Linda, wrote to the *London Firefighter Magazine* in the spring 1988 edition, saying:

There are few words adequate enough to allow me to fully express my feelings to all those people who have shown such kindness and given such support since Colin died... your letters, condolences, the flowers, the generosity of spirit have all been overwhelming.

He was later posthumously awarded the George Medal for his gallant actions.

The family of homeless man Ralph Humberstone has never been traced. He was identified by a publican in Dalston, East London, where he had worked as a cleaner some time before the fire. His body remains in East Finchley Cemetery.

Body 115 was eventually identified in January 2004. Police Inspector Ian Wilkinson was determined to solve the mystery before he left the force, perhaps motivated by criticism levelled at him at the public inquiry for first saying the fire was extinguished, then saying it was 'blazing fiercely'. When he

appeared before the inquiry he admitted he 'did not appreciate the seriousness of the fire until much later on'.

Body 115's skull was reconstructed by forensic scientists
using the remaining bone fragments and clay. It was discovered that a small piece of his skull had been removed during
brain surgery a while before the fire, and a unique 'Sugita'
metal clip had been inserted. He was 73-year-old Alexander
Fallon, a Scot who became a drifter after the death of his wife
in 1973. He was survived by two daughters, Mary Leisham
and Ena Logan, who had assumed he wanted to break all
contact with them. In June 2004, his body was exhumed from
East Finchley Cemetery and he was re-buried alongside his
wife in Falkirk, Scotland.

Margaret Thatcher's government appointed the barrister
Desmond Fennell to conduct the public inquiry into the
King's Cross fire, a decision initially described by some of the
press and members of the political opposition as controversial,
because it was thought that a high court judge would be
chosen. He was also an active member of the Conservative
party. The day Desmond Fennell was appointed he went
down to the seat of the fire to see the destruction for himself.

Fennell's report to Conservative Transport Secretary Paul
Channon was published 'by command of Her Majesty' on 21
October 1988. It made 157 recommendations, the details of
which were made public on 11 November 1988.

Desmond Fennell was praised for being so outspoken about
the failings of London Underground and the performance of
the emergency services on the night of the disaster, and he
went on to become a high court judge in 1990.

The King's Cross fire was without a doubt the worst fire
ever on the Underground, and Fennell's report subsequently
changed safety procedures on the Tube, led to new legislation,

and improved firefighting techniques.

But two decades after the King's Cross fire he expressed his shock and anger to me as I sat in his house on a freezing November morning, that some of his recommendations had still not been implemented: 'we can put a man on the moon, but even now it's still not possible for emergency crews to talk to each other underground.' He recalled the scene that confronted him at the torched station: 'it was like going down into a bloody hell...'

CHAPTER 4

Spencer Park

The sound of the phone ringing echoed against the wooden floor. I picked up the receiver, which was resting on a table piled with a stack of telephone directories in the hallway of my parents' house, where I was living.

'Hello?'

It was Amy, my on-off girlfriend. 'You were there, weren't you?'

'Yes. How did you know?'

'I didn't, but it's like a sixth sense. I just knew you were there. What was it like?'

'It was carnage. There were trapped bodies, and I've never seen so much blood.'

'I just knew it. How are you, darling?'

'I'm OK. It's fine. Everything's fine. It's over now,' I replied.

'It sounds terrible, but everything is OK, sweetheart?'

'Yes, thanks.' The conversation petered out. She knew I didn't really want to talk. We said goodbye and I hung up.

It was a rare week, one of those when I went to work with the majority of Londoners at 9am on a Monday morning. I'd been on leave the previous four days, and had had a busy weekend out drinking with friends on Saturday and going to a family christening on the Sunday.

It was Monday 12 December 1988, and I was 22 years old. I'd been at Stratford for over three years now, with a brief spell of temporary promotion the previous summer at Chingford. Station Officer Tom Harries was still in charge of the Red Watch. I arrived at the station around eight that morning just as the Green Watch were coming to the end of their tour of duty. I chatted to Les, who was at the end of his shift, and stood against the radiator in the watch room waiting for six bells. It was comforting, warm enough to rest on without being too hot as outside it was chilly. I stood in the same place that I had stood just before my 21st birthday and the terrible tragedy of King's Cross a year before. But on this day all I could think of was Christmas and having some time off. I was at the start of my penultimate tour of duty before the festive season and was looking forward to a long break and a party at a pub in Hackney on Christmas Eve; Amy was coming with one of her friends. *Just eight more shifts*, I thought.

Twelve miles away, in southwest London, a commuter train travelling from Basingstoke in Hampshire was approaching Clapham Junction Railway Station. It was one of the busiest intersections in Europe with about 180 trains per hour en route to Central London stations Vauxhall, Waterloo and Victoria. The Basingstoke train departed at 07:18 hours. It was followed by the 06:14 from Poole on the south coast; both trains, which were made up of 12 carriages, were destined for Waterloo. They were between Earlsfield Station and Clapham Junction, a distance of just over one-and-a-half miles, much of which was in a cutting about 50 feet beneath street level. At peak times, a train enters the cutting, parallel to a road, every two minutes. There were two pairs of tracks and the Basingstoke and Poole trains were on the 'up main line'.

At 08:03, a third train left Waterloo heading towards Haslemere, in Surrey on the 'down main line' that ran alongside the other tracks in the opposite direction away from

London; there were no passengers on this train. For the last mile of the line towards Clapham the tracks descend further into the cutting with a gentle turn to the left.

There were two signals on the approach to Clapham Junction: WF47 directly outside the station, and further down the line WF138. At around 08:10, the driver of the Poole train, John Rolls, passed signal WF138, which showed it was safe to proceed, but his view ahead was obstructed by the steep embankment and the curve of the track.

Travelling at around 60 miles an hour, he could see the stationary Basingstoke train in front of him and despite applying the emergency brake, he collided with it. The impact caused the front three carriages of the Poole train to derail, pushing them on to the down main line track opposite. Witnesses later said the noise was like a 'loud explosion.'

As it derailed it careered into the path of the train travelling in the opposite direction to Haslemere but hit it with a 'glancing blow', so despite being derailed, it remained upright. However, the force of the impact was so strong that it pushed the last carriage of the Basingstoke train off the tracks and onto the top wall of the embankment, about ten feet vertically above the tracks. Eight carriages from both trains were either crushed, torn open or completely destroyed in the fatal collision as debris flew into the air, a large cloud of dust rising above the wreckage. The two trains that had been travelling in the same direction became a tangled mess. There were no trains on the remaining two lines to the east of the up and down main; there were 1,500 passengers on the Poole and Basingstoke trains.

A fourth train, travelling towards Clapham behind the Poole train, also cleared signal WF138, so the driver thought it was safe to proceed, but once through the faulty signal, he could see the wrecked Poole train and stopped with about 60 yards to spare.

The crash occurred at peak time, on a busy sunny Monday morning. To the west of the cutting was Emanuel School, from which pupils later came to assist the injured commuters who were in full view of the public. The whole disaster unfolded in a matter of seconds.

At 08:13 the first London Fire Brigade crews were mobilised. Temporary Station Officer Glyn Mills was riding in charge of Battersea's pump. In charge of the pump ladder was Temporary Sub Officer Steve Williams. Additional crews were mobilised: the pump ladder from Tooting; Norbury's emergency rescue tender; a forward control unit was deployed from South West Area Headquarters at Clapham, and an area control unit from Paddington. Two senior officers were dispatched by car: Assistant Divisional Officer Young and Divisional Officer Crompton. The teleprinter slip read: 'Train crash, just prior to Clapham Junction Railway Station, Spencer Park, Wandsworth.' There were another five calls and the control room notified Battersea's crews. Meanwhile, more calls were being received by the Metropolitan Police at the Information Room at New Scotland Yard, and the London Ambulance Service's Headquarters in Waterloo.

At 08:17 Battersea's pump booked in over the radio, followed a minute later by Battersea's pump ladder. Station Officer Mills sent a further four radio messages:

08:18 'From Station Officer Mills at Spencer Park. Make pumps eight.'

08:19 'Make ambulances eight.'

08:20 'Request attendance of surgical unit.'

He sent his first assessment of the incident at 08:21: 'Two trains in collision, unknown number of persons involved.'

Station Officer Mills directed his crews to cut away the railings that separated the road, Spencer Park, from the steep embankment, and although he was not sure if the power was off, he ordered those passengers able to walk to leave the area. The railway tracks into Clapham used the 660-volt third-rail system to power trains – there were no overhead wires, but the electrified rail was lethal if stepped on. Many of the injured weren't aware of this, and it wasn't clear whether the power was off. Fortunately it had short-circuited due to the derailment, preventing electrocution to those already hurt, and protecting passengers who were otherwise uninjured.

At 08:27 the scale of the disaster facing Officer Mills and his firefighters was becoming apparent. He called the control room on the radio: 'This is a major incident – implement major incident procedure.' Two minutes later he requested the number of emergency rescue crews to be made-up to three.

In the watch room at Stratford six bells sounded. It was nine o'clock and news had reached us that a major incident had been declared. We paraded for roll call as normal, but there were no live TV news channels so we knew nothing of the initial call or the drama that was unravelling south of the river.

Once the major incident had been declared, teleprinter messages were circulated to every fire station with updates from the crash. At 08:39 the teleprinter bell sounded in the watch room at Stratford with a transcript of the latest information: 'Two commuter trains in collision, five carriages involved, approximately 150 casualties, unknown number of people trapped, efforts being made to release.'

I didn't think we would get called on. A year earlier I'd stood in the watch room convincing myself that we would get called to the King's Cross Fire. The train crash was miles away – and the south side of the river, much further than King's Cross.

At 08:48 Assistant Chief Officer Ash assumed command of the incident and sent the radio message: 'Make pumps 12 – additional appliances to carry cutting equipment.' Shortly afterwards came the message, 'Make pumps 15,' bringing the number of firefighters at the incident to around 100.

After roll call we sat in the mess as usual and had a cup of tea. Our day-to-day routine continued while we monitored events in Clapham on the appliance radio and teleprinter. The atmosphere at the station was buzzing as messages were relayed from Spencer Park and we talked about what our Green Watch colleagues might be going through, and whether it was serious enough to make it onto the lunchtime news. Then a message was sent to every station restricting the movement of appliances. Stations scheduled to go on inspections, school visits or any other outside duty were ordered to cancel, while senior officers at the Central Operations Room at Brigade Headquarters in Lambeth monitored the incident and kept track of where all their machines were.

At 09:18 a message requesting '48 Acro Props' – sets of strong adjustable poles that can support damaged structures – was sent from Spencer Park, and then at 09:51 another update:

'Three trains involved – eight coaches damaged. Fifty casualties removed to date, a number of casualties still trapped – heavy British Rail road crane ordered from site,' followed by '15 live casualties still on site and a number of dead casualties trapped.'

The initial call to the brigade came in at 08:13. The Green Watch should have completed its tour of duty at 09:00, so as well as having now worked 48 hours in four days, they were well into their second hour of overtime in stressful and demanding conditions after a long night shift. Even the most experienced firefighter would have been shocked by the horrific nature of such a job, with more than 100 injured and several dead. One firefighter later told the public inquiry into the crash that he removed a torso 'wrapped in a blanket, attached to a stretcher'.

At 10:25 ACO McMillan asked for fresh Red Watch Crews to take over from their Green Watch colleagues, who were on the verge of exhaustion: 'Request 18 pump relief, 10 station officers as soon as possible. To approach from Trinity Road and into Windmill Road and rendezvous at junction of Windmill Road and Spencer Road.'

The teleprinter bell sounded at Stratford, but no call bells followed. The duty man, Bob, casually walked to the watch room and acknowledged the message. There was a long list of machines ordered to report to Spencer Park from stations all over the brigade: Feltham, Millwall, Clerkenwell, Kensington, Walthamstow and Shoreditch; the list went on, and then I heard Bob yell from the watch room.

'The pump's going to Spencer Park – governor in charge. Immediate relief.'

I couldn't believe what I was hearing. *That's us*, I thought. *Christ, I'm riding the pump! We're going to the train crash.* I walked into the watch room expecting it to be a joke. I looked at the message on the yellowy roll of teleprinter paper: '18 pump relief, 10 Station Officers: F21's pump, station officer-in-charge.' I was assigned to the pump with Bert Lewinton. Tom Harries was in charge and Gary was driving.

'OK. Get yourselves ready,' said Tom calmly as he walked into the watch room. As it was a relief, we would drive to Clapham at normal speed and without blue lights.

'Are you having your sandwich?' asked Bert.

'Not sure,' replied Tom.

'I think I'll leave it,' I said.

'Could be a while before we get a chance to eat again,' said Bert. I was buzzing with excitement and expectation.

Gary looked up the route in an atlas, Bert walked out of the watch room and upstairs to the mess.

We left the station pretty quickly after Bob phoned the control room and booked us 'mobile to Spencer Park'. We climbed onto the pump and pulled on our fire gear. Then Bert produced a cheese-and-onion sandwich from his pocket and began to eat it.

I was in the hands of some of the most experienced firefighters at Stratford, and as we headed towards central London and over the Bow Flyover, Tom gave a short blast on the siren to speed our way through a hold-up in the traffic. I was sitting on the back of the pump on the offside, Bert to my left.

'Don't worry, Cliff, but you're probably going to see a few sights when we get there. Quite a few stiffs. Try not to worry about it.'

'Thanks, Bert. I don't really know what to expect.'

'Neither do I – none of us do yet. There will be lots of people with crush injuries, but probably only the dead left to deal with by the time we book in.'

'I'll be fine.'

I don't know how long it took to reach Spencer Park, I was disoriented by the journey and had to stand up and peer through the bulkhead behind Gary and the governor to see ahead. We crossed into south London, and I felt like we were miles away from Stratford, but still a long way from the crash as the machine rolled through a series of shortcuts and side roads. I'd never been to a job so far off our ground. Tom knew the area quite well, so we cut through Clapham and took a detour around Battersea to avoid the congested traffic and soon we reached Spencer Road, which was at right angles to Spencer Park. As we pulled up, I could see cranes being used by TV companies to get aerial pictures of the crash site, and a mass of people and machines spread across a grassy triangle next to Spencer Park.

We parked up and Tom took our nominal roll board, a piece of plastic with our names written on it, in a sheet-metal case. He handed the board to an officer through a sliding window on the side of the control unit so the senior officers who were gathering on it knew the name and rank of every firefighter at the incident. Each nominal roll board was slotted into a much bigger board inside the control unit so at a glance they knew how many of each type of machine was at work.

At 11:21 a message was sent: 'Three live casualties are still trapped.' But even though we were now at the scene, we were not put to work until the Green Watch crews were withdrawn. We waited by the control unit. We couldn't see the crash scene, which was across the grass, down an embankment, and below us in a cutting. But we could see firefighters clambering up to the top of the embankment, wearing green high visibility plastic jackets over their tunics. Their faces were black with grease and streaked with sweat. One firefighter staggered to the top, his legs giving way as he fell to the ground, completely spent of energy. He was dragged away to an ambulance by some of his watch-mates, but it was a distressing image: they looked like World War I soldiers emerging from the trenches.

We were keen to start work, so we took some tools and headed towards the crash site. Council workers had cut away bushes, trees and fencing to make the embankment accessible;

it was the only way down to the crash. There was so much going on, and being so close to the wreckage, it was impossible to work out what had happened. I stepped onto the roof of the Basingstoke train. The first thing I saw was a silver foil blanket and my heart sank, knowing there was probably a dead body under the shiny shroud.

There were rescue crews from Euston, Beckenham and Lewisham; their station call-signs stamped onto the reflective jackets in black paint. One of them looked up at me, then got on his hands and knees, pulled back the aluminium blanket and looked behind it. 'We're leaving this one – wrapped right around the bogey. Waiting for another jack.' I nodded in acknowledgement.

The four of us climbed down the ladder and into the gap that was now occupied by three trains next to each other, compressed into a space where there should only be two. It was difficult to move around and fully understand what happened; time collapsed. We were told there were five bodies remaining in the wreckage and to stand by to remove them. Tom and Gary worked their way into a small space to help release a man who was trapped upright in a toilet on the Poole train. A senior officer told me to climb up the short section of ladder and wait for a body. There were four of us standing on the roof of the Basingstoke train and I heard voices from below.

'OK, everyone. Stand by: body coming.'

I didn't know the firefighters who appeared with the body of a young woman. She was stripped down to her underwear, which was ripped to shreds. I felt sad at such an undignified sight, and wished we could cover her up. I don't know whether she was killed by the impact or died from her injuries, but the crews working below me carefully laid her out. She was placed into a white plastic body bag, which was zipped up and then tied to a short piece of aluminium ladder, used as a makeshift stretcher. We lowered a rope and pulled her up. I hauled the line with all my strength as we grabbed the temporary stretcher, bringing the woman's body to waist height, then passed her on to the next crew above us, who were standing on the lower edge of the embankment. The whole operation took several minutes. Despite the December cold I was hot, but calm, immersed in the action.

I didn't know who she was, or where she was from, but I was struck by the sight of someone's daughter, wife or girlfriend being lifted from the wreckage with barely a scrap of clothing to preserve her dignity. I couldn't imagine how she'd felt that morning: getting up for work, laying out her clothes, then sitting on the train thinking about her journey to Waterloo, perhaps her mind wandered off to think about someone she loved, or what she had planned for the week ahead. The impact must have been terrible to have thrown her around with such force and leave her in that state.

This experience was also different to the fatal fires I'd been to where victims were completely distorted by the heat and flames, virtually unrecognisable. But this woman appeared as though she'd been attacked by a gang, or pack of animals, who'd ripped at her clothes.

As my sense of time dissolved, I began to realise how little I really knew about what was going on. The larger the incident, the harder it was to have an overall picture of what was happening, and what everyone else around us was doing. We were just focused on our own task, a small link in the chain. We didn't have personal radios, so we only heard by word of mouth what was going on. I knew Gary and Tom were still working to free the trapped man, but I never saw that body come out. We knew we were down to the last few bodies and that there was no one alive in the wreckage. Standing on the roof of the rear carriages of the Basingstoke train, a temporary bridge from track level, I had an aerial view of the operation beneath me, which I surveyed with a strange sense of detachment.

A group of firefighters was huddled beneath me and a second body was dragged along then tipped forwards into the upright position. He was a young man, probably in his thirties, and as the crews below me pushed him, his head dropped forwards. His face was covered in blood, made sticky as it coagulated, and his hair was dark, possibly from the grease or dirt disturbed from the trains by the impact. His skull was severely fractured from directly behind the top of his forehead to just above the lowest section of vertebral bone. It looked to me like a cracked boiled egg, as if someone had slipped with the spoon and cut it open at an oblique angle. I couldn't tell whether his brain was intact under the blood, which was so bright it was almost fluorescent, or whether it was dislodged in the impact. The wound was very deep. I'd never seen anything like it.

He was fully dressed in a sweater and dark trousers. He was placed in a body bag and as I hauled him up onto the carriage. I could feel his chilled skin, like a frozen joint of meat, through the thin white plastic as I grappled the makeshift stretcher and handed the body to the crew above me.

At 14:36, a message was sent from the crash to the control room: 'Steady progress being maintained in extricating remaining bodies.' Around the same time we were ordered to leave the crash scene. We stood by Stratford's pump, trying to work out why the machine was missing half its equipment. A pile of dumped tools lay in the middle of a makeshift camp built on a disaster that was occupied by hundreds of emergency workers. The bare triangle of grass in Spencer Park, adjacent to the tracks, had in a few hours been turned into an urban war zone. I was at the front.

Tom told us to go to the Round House pub nearby to use the toilets, (we were not normally allowed in a pub in fire gear). All the main roads, including the busy road from south London to Hampshire, were closed. I walked in through a side door and headed to the toilets, which were down the hallway, avoiding walking through the bar. I stood at one of the urinals and removed my helmet, then my tunic so I could lower my leggings. I tried to absorb what I'd seen, a unique sight witnessed by few, but my thoughts were broken by a man who walked into the toilet and stood at the urinal to my right. He looked like a regular in the pub.

'What's it like there, mate? We've been watching on the telly.'

'Pardon?' I asked.

'The crash – pretty serious isn't it? I bet you've seen some sights.'

I was jolted back into the real world, now distant from the awful disaster, to a pre-Christmas pub at lunchtime where the locals watched the disaster on television.

I replied politely without giving away too much. 'It's very serious.' But what I was really thinking was, *Why don't you fuck off and mind your own business*? All I wanted to do was talk to the other rescuers about what I'd seen, knowing we'd all understand each other.

He persisted. 'We've been watching it on the BBC and ITN lunchtime news.'

I wasn't interested in the fact that it was on national news: I didn't want to watch it on TV, I wanted to get back to the crash site and help find the remaining bodies.

'I bet you could murder a pint,' said the man.

'I can't drink on duty. Please... excuse me.'

It made me realise that even though the pub was just a few feet from such tragedy, for some people, life went on. Everyone becomes an expert, or have an opinion on the cause and extent of the injuries in a disaster, but actually getting involved in the day-to-day job of picking up the pieces was beyond most.

I left the pub and returned to Bert and the others. We were sent back down to the crash site and this time I walked along a section of track with Gary. I was back in the moment, trying hard to take in what I'd seen. I felt a sense of achievement. I'd got involved, helped out, ferrying kit up and down the embankment. I'd seen some truly awful sights, but I was just getting on with it. Any thoughts of Christmas, or plans for the all-night party, and of Amy, were all swept aside as I focused on this incident, the biggest I'd ever attended.

Gary had spotted a piece of brain tissue on one of the rails, which I looked at closely. I thought perhaps it had been picked up from the ballast and placed directly on the thick steel track for safe keeping. I contemplated how awful the scene must have been five or six hours earlier, with scores of people wandering around in shock, with so many casualties, and how traumatic it was for the firefighters who had to place the bodies in the temporary mortuary near the grassy patch.

Then the order was given for us to return to the ladder at the foot of the Basingstoke train as the final body was about to be removed. A rescue crew was using jacks and cutting equipment that was only carried on their machines. The crews gathered around the last body, which was trapped under a bogey of one of the carriages of the Haslemere train; it had been pushed off the rails but remained upright. The emergency rescue tender firefighters removed the aluminium blanket that was covering the wheels of the train, where there was a body underneath. It had somehow become wound around the axle and wedged in the very small gap above the wheels but beneath the underside of the carriage. It looked as though the man had been thrown from a carriage of the Poole train and landed under the Haslemere train passing in the opposite direction. The crew used jacks to lift the axle from the rails, and to open the space between the bogey and the carriage above.

I waited in position for the body to be released. One of the crews laid it out and I was amazed at what I saw: a man, stripped of every single piece of clothing and covered from head to toe in thick black grease. He had large tears to his skin where it was ripped open, but his bony framework was intact – he hadn't lost any limbs, but it was as though he'd been slung onto a butcher's hook and dipped in boiling tar then hung out to dry. If the earlier sight of the woman in her torn underwear was shocking for its lack of dignity, this was far worse. It was impossible to tell his age and with no other clothing or personal possessions, he was also stripped of his identity. His was the final body to be removed.

I'd only played a very small part, but I wanted to know who these people were. This was a disaster, however, so huge in scale that it was impossible. It was frustrating not knowing the full extent of what was going on, and I felt the responsibility of handling the dead, whose loved ones possibly didn't even know their fate. I treated them with care and looked after them as best I could.

I later learned that the Clapham train crash was attended by 243 London Fire Brigade personnel. The initial emergency escalated to 15 pumps with an additional 18-pump relief. A further six-pump relief were ordered at 13:31 to be 'in attendance' for 15:00. There was one further informative message at 15:52: 'All bodies now removed from remaining coaches. British Rail heavy cutting and lifting units in operation. Brigade crews now standing by.'

We handed over the final body and our task was complete. I felt a peculiar sense of satisfaction from this extraordinary job as we returned to Stratford in time for the end of our shift at six in the evening.

The incident was concluded by a message transmitted from the control unit at 16:50: 'Stop for Spencer Park. Two passenger trains of 12 coaches in collision in cutting south of Clapham Junction Railway Station. One hundred and thirteen persons injured, 35 apparently dead. Holmatro and cold-cutting equipment. Thermal image camera. All persons not yet accounted for.'

The brigade kept a presence at the crash until the following day. At 10:03 the message 'All persons accounted for' was sent, then at 12:10: 'Brigade attendance no longer required at this incident. All gear made up with the exception of a line being used as a handrail, which will be returned by police.'

I kept a diary. For Monday 12 December, I wrote: 'Rode pump, got ordered as an immediate relief to the train crash at Spencer Park, Wandsworth, outside Clapham. Spent the day ferrying equipment used to free bodies. Assisted four bodies out of wreckage, 35 people died and over a hundred were injured.' The entry illustrates the extent to which I had switched off, only recording the barest of details of what happened, almost in shorthand. The scale of the disaster was registering but I couldn't articulate it. I was giving everyone a factual account of what happened without conveying my feelings. Perhaps it was more about scoring points: with other firefighters, my family and friends. Being heroic meant being cool, not showing any emotion. I was well paid for what I did, it was the job I loved and I just craved the next shift and the next callout. Nothing was too big, too serious or too frightening for me. The memory of the fourth body has been inexplicably erased from my mind, buried deep into my subconscious.

Two things really struck me about the Clapham crash. The first was the conversation with Amy that evening. It was her sixth sense at work, knowing and feeling that I'd been there. It was impossible to predict this disaster. But it escalated quickly and with devastating consequences the very second the Poole train crashed into the train in front.

The second was the sense of detachment, suddenly being launched into the most bizarre scenario. The next day I rode the pump again at Stratford. It was a busy day; we had five shouts, I wrote in my diary that I had 'spent the evening unwinding'. I was only 22, and looking back, realise now just how young I was, but having joined the job at 18, I didn't really know any different. I had learned what to do after experiencing such tragedies, how to block out the horrors, but they were there, hidden below the surface with the potential for torment to rise in the future. Not only was I getting the hit or the high of the 'drug' of danger and adrenaline, but I was getting the aftershock as well. My relationships were suffering. I wasn't settled or committed. I socialised a lot, but mainly during the week so I missed out on countless parties, weddings and Christmas celebrations – the work always came first. But away from work, without a close family or steady relationship, I was often lost.

The weekend after the Clapham train crash I drove to see Amy. It was a long journey from Redbridge to Roehampton in southwest London, where she lived. I was going to see her for the first time since the crash. I had drifted apart from Colette, my previous girlfriend, after a few years together. She had moved to a different hospital in northwest London and I was stuck between not being able to commit to a relationship or actually ending it. Instead I hid behind my job, which was always my first priority. I was also obsessed with being independent, in charge of my life and my career.

I had started seeing Amy at the end of 1987 and we started going out in 1988, but if I was not committed to Colette, then I was even less so with Amy. It was a turbulent relationship and we'd go through phases of not talking and not seeing each other. But she genuinely empathised with me being at the train crash. It was 17 December, and I was looking forward to Christmas to take my mind off things and Spencer Park. The shifts after the crash had been busy, but what I'd witnessed had been dumped into my mental filing cabinet as the next emergency overrode the one before.

I crossed the river in my car and headed through south London towards Amy's. I'd made the trip countless times and as I drove around Clapham Common. I thought about how much I was looking forward to seeing her. We had plans to go to an Italian restaurant in South Kensington that night. I passed through Clapham and into Battersea Rise. It was quite a fast stretch of road and within a minute I was crossing a set of four railway lines but couldn't see the tracks because of the high sides of the brick-built bridge. Then it all felt very familiar. There on my right was the Round House pub.

I was back at Spencer Park, where I'd carefully manoeuvred the bodies, examined a brain on the track, entered the pub and been polite to a man I really wanted to punch. I stopped the car between the tracks and the grass. It was cold, dark and eerie. I couldn't believe it, I was on the road where the control unit had been parked. It was a massive shock, not only because I was unexpectedly back at the heart of the tragedy within less than a week, but because I'd driven over the bridge countless times. A week before, I was so wrapped up in the drama that I had no idea that I was close to Amy's flat as we pulled up at Spencer Park. Not only had the disaster taken away my sense of the real world, it had taken away my sense of location. The road had been closed a week earlier, but now hundreds of cars were driving past the scene of so much pain, their occupants oblivious to the recent destruction.

I began to relive the moment. I found the fence where we'd accessed the embankment that led down to the side of the track, which had now been repaired. The trains were passing by at full speed and there were only a few flowers to suggest there had even been a disaster.

Fucking hell, I thought. *I'm back here – with no one to watch my back. Just me the dark and the memory of death.* An icy shiver ran down my spine. I felt naked and vulnerable without my uniform and suddenly very alone. I tried to make sense of my disorientation. *I've been here loads of times. Why didn't I realise that last week?*

It was Tom Harries expert knowledge of London's roads that had disoriented me the week before. He guided our driver Gary through Battersea so we came via a circuitous route – and from the north of Spencer Park. Most machines coming from north of the river stuck to the main roads: the South Circular and the A3. But taking the route we did, we didn't cross the Battersea Rise bridge, and the roads had been closed and blocked by scores of vehicles.

In the dark, I walked across the grass towards the railway embankment. It was also impossible to see down to the crash site from the pavement. I stood in the same position where, days earlier, I'd seen a Green Watch colleague collapse under the strain of what he'd experienced. I looked at the temporary path cleared to allow us access, the spot where so many bodies once freed from the wreckage were brought up to street level, ahead of the long process of identifying them, checking their possessions and contacting their loved ones – the bad news delivered to many families so close to Christmas.

It was scary and shocking: a place I knew, but for one day had looked so different. I got in my car, drove off and met Amy. Another date, another dinner, another woman who was prepared to listen and perhaps help me pick up the pieces, even if I didn't know how to myself.

The week after, I drank myself through the night at a Christmas Eve party, locked in the Albion pub in Hackney with Amy and a friend. I drank whisky and was so ill I was still recovering on Boxing Day.

Amy and I eventually drifted apart. But I loved the company of women, and fell into a cycle of repeatedly starting new relationships. There was always someone to hear my stories and that attention added to the addiction as I craved the next job like a junkie does his next fix. I was convinced that nothing could go wrong. But the tragedies and the half-committed relationships were beginning to erode something deep in my mind as the triangle began to bend out of shape.

CHAPTER 5

Flashover

The call bells rang and all the fire station's lights came on. I jumped out of the iron bed wedged against the wall of the watch room, pulled on my boots and hoisted up the padded blue overtrousers, slipping the braces over my shoulders.

The call was to a fire in a mini-cab office, Church Street, off West Ham Lane. I punched the button on the shiny new control box fixed to the wall to acknowledge the call, then pressed two buttons that lit the red and green light bulbs in the appliance bay deploying both pump and pump ladder.

It was the early hours of a Sunday morning and through the darkness we reached the fire in a few minutes. The cab office had a large glass shop window, to its left an entrance door, and directly behind there was a waiting area for customers. The office was closed, it was eerily quiet and the glass glowed from behind a shade of sunset orange. There was little smoke and hardly any sign of fire. It felt too quiet.

Bob and I climbed from the pump ladder in our breathing apparatus, took a hose reel and entered the door, immediately disappearing into thick, low-rolling smoke. It was very hot, my ears tingled and we pulled open the lever on the hose reel to knock back the fire and smoke, the water turned to superheated steam. We were about 10ft inside the entrance when there was a thunderous explosion. A ferocious flaming ball shot through a gap in a screen intended to let customers talk to the cab office controller, while protecting him or her from possible attack. The small hole had the effect of pressurising the gases like a nozzle, the force overwhelming Bob and me. Outside there was a loud clang. Roger had broken the 10ft by 8ft pane of glass at the front of the office to vent the fire, but it was too late to prevent the fire from erupting because of the sudden addition of air to fuel it. There was a *whoosh* past my ears and I was blown to the floor inside the cab office - Bob was ejected, flying like a rugby scrum-half into the street.

'On your feet! Back on your fucking feet!' yelled Peter the Sub Officer.

'Are you OK?' someone shouted. We were unable to speak, our faces encased in our masks. We got up and grabbed the hose reel. A jet of water was being aimed through the large opening where the window had been from outside.

'Get your set on, Pete!' I heard Tom Harries shout. I thought, *This is serious for the governor to send an officer in with us.* The three of us pushed forwards and knocked the fire down but the entire office was destroyed.

I'd experienced some pretty hot and serious fires, but nothing of this force, and the office was only about 10ft wide by 15ft deep. It was my first flashover.

The fire service had changed. The World War II teleprinters had been replaced by a computer printer. The paper was bright white, and stacked in a box as opposed to being wound in a roll. Our uniform had changed too. The yellow vinyl overtrousers were replaced by heavier padded blue ones, and the traditional wool tunic made way for a longer bunker-style coat with a zip front covered by a Velcro flap, also in blue. The combed cork helmet was no more, but replaced by a modern Kevlar version with a clear visor that could be pulled down. The new tunic was much longer and couldn't take an axe and belt, so these were stored in lockers on the machines. Traditionally the axe was a personal item of equipment, although not in my time.

The changes were a consequence of the King's Cross fire. The traditional fire rig was based on something very close to what was worn by our Edwardian forebears. We now had fireproof neckerchiefs, leather gloves that came up to the wrist, and a protective cuff on the sleeve of the tunic. Our ears were still exposed, and we were testing a radio that could be used while wearing breathing apparatus. I knew firefighters who had served 20 years, some with pockmarked skin on their necks caused by burns. I'd heard stories of firefighters who had fought blazes in the holds of ships in Royal Docks, their hands burned and scarred as they climbed up fixed metal ladders when they could fight the blaze no more.

But our attitude to firefighting did not change. We tackled the beast at its heart. We considered ourselves too professional to stand outside a job and simply pour water in, besides which the damage can equal and even possibly be worse than that caused by the fire.

The extreme adrenaline rush that came from such fires compared with nothing else I knew. Improved equipment meant we felt even more indestructible, our bodies could take more punishment in the harshest of conditions, and I was building up a good track record of some tough working jobs.

One spring Sunday night we were sent from Stratford as part of a large relief to a cold store that had been on fire since the previous night. It was in Charterhouse Street in the City of London. The store was owned by the Port of London Authority, and was adjacent to Smithfield meat market but had lain derelict for many years. We were told we would be working our way into the fire along about 100ft of hose, which had a large ground monitor attached to it. The monitor could be left in place; it stood on a base so did not need to be held by firefighters. But the angle and direction of the jet of water needed regular repositioning so it could be aimed at the fire.

For such a large store, it only had a narrow passage – about the same size as a terraced house. I was working with Roger Laker and a station officer from Shoreditch who told us to follow him.

'You can't wear a set,' he said. 'No point. You'll be out of air by the time you reach the monitor and the fire.' I was about to embark on some old-fashioned firefighting, referred to by the experienced hands as 'smoke-eating'.

We walked along the passage, leaning forwards so our faces were closer to the fresher air lower down. It was dark but for a temporary spotlight in the distance as we inched along, following the hose. The atmosphere was like a very hot sauna until we were several hundred feet into the building. Every gasp of air was hot and tingled on the back of my throat, sweat poured from my skin, soaking my uniform from my neck to my socks, with steam gathering in the creases. We reached the heavy ground monitor that had been left in place, pumping out thousands of gallons of water. The three of us lifted the ground monitor and pushed further forwards. About 30ft ahead of us, the passage opened out and we could see a glowing crucible but the smoke was also much heavier so we crouched low, keeping our faces about six inches off the ground as we gasped for what little clean air there was. The monitor repositioned, we retreated, the whole exercise taking about 45 minutes as the water from the monitor very slowly extinguished the fire.

When we reached the outside of the building, the cool fresh

air hit us. We crossed the road and slumped on to the pavement, leaning against the wall of one of the meat market's warehouses and looking back at the smoke that was still rising out of the roof from the fire. We'd been there a few hours, and I was so exhausted my thighs felt as though they'd been stripped of every fibre of muscle and replaced with jelly. I was close to collapse and I felt disoriented. My hands shook but it was impossible to see them through blurred vision.

We were sent to the canteen van for a cup of tea and a fish-paste sandwich. The Salvation Army had for many years provided the LFB with a mobile catering service that was used at big fires to refresh exhausted crews and provide some measure of pastoral care – it was always a very welcome sight. The service still operates today, running out of Shoreditch Fire Station, where the City and Hackney boroughs meet. Whenever I hear the Salvation Army playing carols at Christmas, I always stop to make a donation, and pause to reflect for a moment.

The Charterhouse Street store kept meat fresh by insulating it in a cold but non-refrigerated store and had been decommissioned many years earlier. The interior walls were lined with massive cork walls about a foot thick, coated in bitumen. This provided plenty of fuel for the fire, but also kept it well-insulated, making it extremely hot. We returned to Stratford after a couple of hours, and I was still feeling the effects of heat exhaustion, so the governor told me to take a salt tablet, dissolve it in water and drink to rehydrate me and build up my strength. They were known as cooling-draught tablets and we kept a jar in the stores. We still had the rest of the night shift ahead of us.

The exertion, the physical strength and courage needed for such fires made my job all the more appealing. I was revelling in the role of being a hard man, equipped to fight against such adversity. These fires were huge emotional and physical tests but we loved it, no matter how punishing.

On our second night shift, we were sent back on relief to Charterhouse Street. The fire had been burning for more than two days but it was nearly out. This time we could walk upright, as far as the seat of the fire where the monitor was just cooling it from much closer than the night before. Recovered from my exhaustion, I felt proud of the small part I'd played in tackling such a huge blaze, but deep inside I was growing restless.

I was sitting on a green cast-iron chair, on the patio of my parents' bungalow. There were a few steps down to the square garden below. I placed a notepad on the table, and down the left-hand side I wrote a list of the years: 1989, 1990, 1991... and so it went on. Then to the right I wrote out where I'd hope to be, and what I'd hope to be doing. I planned my promotion exams, where I'd like to work, and noted that I also wanted to return to college and study law. I sat there and drifted away to a time in the future when I'd be the governor, the one who worked out the strategy for dealing with a big fire: the person everyone else looked up to. But despite three years at Stratford I was still the junior buck. There had been some vacancies on the Red Watch, but they were always filled by firefighters transferring from other stations due to its popularity and there was no recruit from training school.

Some of my contemporaries had stayed JB for only months. For me it was years and I was frustrated by being the baby of the family, still living at home at a time when the prospect of buying property was made impossible by ever-spiralling prices. My parents sold the house in which I was born in

94

Forest Gate in the spring of 1988 for £60,000 and wondered how they'd manage the mortgage on the bungalow bought for £80,000. I liked the bungalow, it was much more suburban than where we lived before, but I felt strangely attached to the house in which I was born. I was a part of it: the place where I'd lit bonfires, my dreams and fantasies carried away on the smoke of the wintry night air. The place where I ran free at the end of the road with its old men, dented cars and games of war.

Outside work I socialised with a group who weren't firefighters. There was a natural respect that came with my status. Some nightclubs let firefighters in for free. I did some part-time driving work for an agency and also worked as a freelance photographer, submitting pictures to local newspapers. Most of the recruiting agency's members were firefighters working on their days off – we were paid extra in cash, and were attractive to women looking for someone responsible, safe and brave.

I sat in the garden in bright sunlight planning my future. There was no limit to what I might land up doing, nothing to hinder my enthusiasm and no one was going to stop me. I was reassured, in that tranquil moment, by the peace of my surroundings, happy with life and looking forward to living my dream.

I remained at Stratford for a couple of years and then, in the spring of 1990, I applied for a transfer out. I also qualified for a flat provided by the Crown Estate Commission, which rented out property to essential workers in London. The Crown Estate managed the thousands of business and residential properties owned by the Queen.

My station commander blocked a swap with a Red Watch

firefighter from Leytonstone but offered a list of alternatives. I had a choice of about five stations, but most were not on the Red Watch, so I'd be working alongside completely new firefighters. After five years at Stratford I'd been to other stations when they were short-staffed all over the area and I was very well known. This would be a new start. I chose the Blue Watch at Kingsland Road in Hackney. The station covered a small area but was very close to the City so offered a new challenge.

In May 1990, aged 23, I was handed the keys to a studio flat with a large kitchen and dining area with a lovely walled courtyard garden, opposite Victoria Park in Bow. In June I emptied my locker at Stratford and was on the move. Shortly after, my replacement on the Red Watch arrived from training school.

By my first shift at Kingsland, I had five years' experience and was immediately offered 'acting up' or temporary promotion to leading firefighter. I was earning good money now and had complete freedom: my own flat, a new area to explore and the added responsibility of leading my own crew.

It was only my second tour of duty, a Friday night, when a fire started in an office block that was being renovated about a mile from the station. I was in charge of the pump ladder. The building was the new Broadgate development, where some years before there had been a railway station by the same name next to Liverpool Street Station. Just after midnight a call came in to a fire: 'Persons reported. Cylinders involved. Broadgate near Bishopsgate.' Kingsland would often take a lot of extra calls as the station had a hydraulic platform that could reach around 100ft in height and play water onto a fire from a large monitor fixed to the cage from where the officer-in-charge worked. It was also used to rescue people from windows and roofs high above the ground. But we hadn't been called yet.

Shortly after the first call, the officer-in-charge of Barbican's machine made the job a four-pumper, and we gathered in the watch room at Kingsland to monitor the messages coming back from the fire. The fire station was just over a mile from the incident, but there were many more stations in the city – Shoreditch, Bethnal Green, Homerton, Dowgate and Islington – each covering a smaller area. Then the bells went down and the pump was dispatched to what had now escalated to a six-pumper. I felt a real urge, a craving to get called on with the pump ladder and my crew. The job escalated further: 'Make pumps 10', then 15 pumps, but we didn't move. The pressure was unbearable with such eagerness to get called and stuck in. I couldn't believe it; we were so close. As teleprinter messages came in I read them and imagined what the other crews were doing. Then over the radio 'make pumps 20,' followed shortly after by the ringing bells. We were on. It was now 01:38 on Saturday, the fire had been burning just over an hour but was far from under control.

As the pump ladder headed towards Bishopsgate I felt an incredible high, a surge in excitement and a huge blast of adrenaline. I'd never been to a fire so big and it was in the City of London, which made it all the more exciting. As the machine approached the job I could see a staff officer from one of the control units frantically waving his arms. I wondered if this was going to be one of those jobs with lots of machines but not much work – overkill, perhaps, by a cautious senior officer. The staff officer directed us into a side road to the right. I wound down the window.

'Get in and back up Shoreditch's pump and pump ladder. They're trying to get a jet to work that end. Be careful: there's cylinders and a partial collapse,' said the staff officer.

'Is it bad?'

'Still two unaccounted for.'

We jumped from the pump ladder and followed a massive tangle of hose, spread out over some ornate stone steps. Shoreditch's governor was trying to bend a length of hose in half in order to release the pressure so the line could be extended. He was a small wiry man and I thought, *Good luck with that – I've never seen anyone successfully break a coupling that way.* I tried to trace the jet of the hose back to the outlet on the pump supplying it. A tag should have been taken off the outlet or tap and hung around the branch of the hose so it was clear from which outlet the pump was supplying which branch, but these things were often overlooked.

My crew broke up and went to help other crews. We weren't wearing breathing apparatus and were working in an open-plan office section. The fire was above us and large sheets of plasterboard dropped in front of us under the weight of water. There were small pockets of fire burning in the voids. We worked all night physically grafting on the lines of hose and jets that began to feel like they were charged with iron, not water.

By the time we returned to the station, it was around five in the morning. There was no point in putting our beds down as we'd soon be getting up. At nine we went off duty, looking forward to four days off. I slept until three and just about made it to the pub for a beer before closing time.

Although I liked Kingsland, the annual round of promotions started a few months later. I applied, knowing that if I was successful it would mean moving again – and I'd have no choice but to be told where I was going. I knew it would be one of the North East Area's 26 stations. Although I'd been a JB for five years, I'd also completed my promotion exams and gained quite a bit of experience as a temporary leading fire-fighter. Substantive promotion meant more money, and a lot more responsibility. I had the interview in November 1990, and then about a week later, I went to visit my parents. I let myself in with a key, and walked through the front door. They were not at home. As I walked past the phone, it rang.

'Is that Clifford?'

'Yes. Who's speaking, please?' I was puzzled because I was not expecting to be called at my parents' house, where I no longer lived.

'Divisional Officer Godfrey. About your promotion: you've been successful. Ilford Green Watch.' The news delivered in routine staccato fashion, like a chattering teleprinter.

'That's great, sir. Thanks very much.'

'We'll sort your paperwork and transfer you in time for Christmas. Well done. You'll have a formal presentation of your rank markings later.'

And so after six months at Kingsland, I was emptying my locker again, this time heading for a suburban station, but one that covered a very big area. Ilford Fire Station lies approximately five miles to the east of Stratford's and they share a border and 'take appliances' onto each other's ground. Ilford has a town centre with a large shopping mall. Its ground is dissected by the M11 motorway and the A406 link road, which connects the M25 via several busy urban intersections. The station covers an area of 22 square kilometres: more than twice the size of Stratford's. Even with improvements to fire safety, today Stratford attends about 1,600 emergency calls, including 500 fires per year. Ilford takes around 1,900, including 560 fires.

I arrived just after my 24th birthday, looking forward to a

new challenge and another set of colleagues with fresh enthusiasm and an ever-present craving to be part of the action.

CHAPTER 6

Gordon

It is 20 December 1991. The Green Watch is on its second night shift, and the last tour of duty before Christmas. Station Officer Bill McGuyver is the officer-in-charge of the watch, and riding the pump. I am a substantive leading firefighter and second-in-command of the station, riding in charge of the pump ladder. I've been at Ilford a year. Just before supper, the bells ring and the teleprinter spits out a message:

21:02 Foxtrot 42 Ilford. F42 Pump Ladder. F42 Pump: fire. People believed inside, opposite 148 Eton Road Ilford.

I run from the station office on the ground floor, through the watch room, where the duty man hands me the call slip shouting, 'Fire! People inside! Eton Road!' I climb into the cab of the pump ladder and as the automatic doors open I jam my foot against the button that operates its sirens on the floor of the cab. The pump rolls through the bay doors ahead of us, both machines turn right into Ilford High Road. The control room calls Station Officer McGuyver on the radio: *21:04 'Foxtrot four-two-two from F-E – we're receiving multiple calls to Eton Road. Persons believed involved. F43 Barking. Pump ladder and pump dispatched additional. Over.'*

I hear the message come in on the pump ladder's radio.

Barking's crews turn left on to the busy A13 dual carriageway at Ripple Road, travelling from their base about a mile-and-a-half south of Eton Road, dispatched before we have reached the fire. Four crews are mobile to the incident. Several occupants of houses surrounding the fire have dialled 999, many giving conflicting house numbers.

We turn, then turn again, right into Eton Road before we pull-up. I pick up the radio telephone handset.

'F-E, Foxtrot four-two-one, Foxtrot four-two-two. Status three. Over.'

A pager sounds with rapid bleeps.

21.06 Mobilising message: Foxtrot four-one: Assistant Divisional Officer Boyce, by pager at F41 Dagenham. Multiple calls. Fire. People believed inside. Opposite 248 Eton Road.

ADO Boyce drives to the incident alone in a red marked brigade car with a single blue light on top. He is travelling from the east, about two miles from the fire.

I climb from the pump ladder. Smoke is punching out of the upstairs bay window at the front of the 1930s terraced house, and from a smaller window to the right from another bedroom. The water supply is engaged on the pump – it has stopped in front of the pump ladder. The engine revs ferociously to ensure there is enough water pressure to knock down the fire. I hear repeated piercing screams from a man and woman standing on the pavement on the opposite side of the road to the fire.

My crew climbs from the pump ladder, they're wearing breathing apparatus.

'Start up! Start up!' I yank their tallies off. 'Get in there! Upstairs, front! Go to the front!' I shout, and run to the pump and pull off the hose reel.

'Let's have the pump's crew rigged. Two men, back room— Cliff, make sure the ladder's crew searches the rooms at the front, and two the rest of the house,' says Station Officer McGuyver.

'OK, guv. Take the tallies. Bob.' I hand them over to the driver of Ilford's pump and follow the first breathing apparatus crew of two into the hall. They're up the stairs and out of sight hidden by the flourishing smoke. Barking's machines arrive and its crews gather outside the house.

21.08 'Station Officer McGuyver at 247 Eton Road. Make pumps four. Persons reported.'

Details of the fire are sent back to all the stations involved in the incident. One minute later the damage-control tender is deployed from its base in Chingford several miles north of the incident. The forward control unit, Foxtrot two-zero-one – a white Range Rover with a row of flashing lights across the top, a sub officer in charge, and a leading firefighter driver – is mobilised from area staff at Stratford, and the Fire Investigation Unit from East Ham is also dispatched.

Station Officer McGuyver is standing in the street facing the burning house. 'I'm going in, guv,' I say. Without breathing apparatus, I go up the stairs of the house dragging a hose reel. I get as close to the top of the stairs as I can – my head is level with the carpet on the landing. I can't go any further without breathing apparatus as the smoke is dense and now percolating down the staircase.

I run down the stairs and grab a coiled reel of 70mm hose, flick it and lay it out as a covering jet to the front elevation of the house. I go back in through the front and up the stairs.

My nostrils flare, I feel the sticky soot hit the lining of my nose, my eyes water furiously. From the outside, smoke and flames are licking the guttering, level with the eaves of the roof. The blackened windows crack and blow out, shards of glass drop into the front garden. I'm at the top of the stairs and I turn left and see a ball of flames and thick black smoke in the front bedroom and hear shouting from one of my breathing-apparatus crew, Firefighter Steve Munday, but I can't get any further into the fire.

There is a layer of thick, highly toxic smoke, diluted by fresh air flowing towards me along the landing, so I take a few steps down the stairs but keep focused on the seat of the fire. I'm crouching but still about level with the carpet on the first floor. Now the smoke is much thicker and rolling along the landing towards me, pushing upwards, powdery black on a convection current but I don't have time to go down the stairs and get my set.

Outside ADO Boyce arrives, books status three or in attendance on the radio, and takes command of the incident from Bill McGuyver.

Steve is running towards me at the top of the stairs with what looks like the body of a child in his arms. 'Got him! Got him!' he yells, breathless words muffled by his face mask. I run down the stairs to the bottom sensing that Steve, with the body and his set on, is too wide for the doorway. I raise my right leg and plant the sole of my boot into the outer porch doors fracturing the glass panels, which drop to the ground with a clang. The wood splinters as the frame gives way making the gap much wider. I turn back towards the bottom of the stairs, and on the doorstep a body is passed to me. It's a small child, a boy – he's unconscious and limp. Over my right shoulder, from the opposite side of the road I hear screaming.

'My baby! Jesus Christ: my baby, PLEASE!'

I kneel on the crazy-paving path and lay the body out in front of me. I flick the switch on my torch and briefly shine it into the body's hollow eyes. I seal my mouth around the tiny red lips and nose of the boy, who looks about two or three years old. It takes a fraction of a breath from my large lungs to inflate the boy's. His chest rises. Station Officer McGuyver is standing above me now, illuminating my actions with a hand-held torch, and then Ilford Firefighter Paul Brightley joins me and starts chest compressions.

'Good, Cliff. Good. Just keep going,' says Bill calmly.

'Is there a pulse? Check for a pulse,' says Graham, one of Ilford's drivers.

'I can feel something very faint – yes, it's faint and rapid,' I reply.

21.11 'From Station Officer McGuyver at 247 Eton Ilford. One child rescued from first floor level, suffering from smoke inhalation. Attempts being made to resuscitate.'

I continue to blow gently into the boy's mouth. Bill crouches and feels the boy's wrist for a pulse, then presses a forefinger under his jaw, on his neck, to locate the carotid pulse.

'Keep going, Cliff. There's definitely something there,' he says.

'Yes, there is something, guv,' I say.

'It feels like a little bird fluttering. Just keep going.'

'Where's the fucking ambulance?' I yell between two breaths.

'It'll be here, Cliff. Just keep on going – keep going, mate!' says Bill.

One of the drivers comes over. 'There's no sign of the ambulance, guv. Control have given us an ETA but can't confirm.'

As details from the fire ground emerge, Divisional Officer Lambell is paged at his base. He is one rank higher than ADO Boyes and is mobilised as the incident escalates, driving an unmarked car with a magnetic blue light on top, he radios his acknowledgement: *'21.19. M-2-F-E, Foxtrot five-seven. Mobile to Eton Road, Ilford. Over.'*

It will take him 22 minutes to reach the incident from his quarters at Poplar Fire Station in the East End.

At the same time, Leytonstone's pump ladder is dispatched to stand by at Ilford, the station now empty for 16 minutes. Dagenham's pump moves to Barking as resources are depleted.

Eton Road, over a mile long, is now blocked for more than a 100 yards along its length. All the machines dispatched on the multiple calls and make up message converge in the narrow side road with cars parked either side of it. The police arrived shortly after us. A 'fast' area car, working out of Ilford Police Station is parked at the head of the static convoy; it is a white Ford Sierra with an orange/red stripe along the side, crewed by two constables.

'Where the fuck are the paramedics, guv? He needs help! We've got to have them now, for fuck sake!' I yell.

'I can take them in the car,' says one of the constables.

'OK, Cliff. Go with the police,' says Bill. I look up. 'Just go. Get him to hospital. We can't wait.'

I pick up the boy. He's still limp as I cradle him in my arms, his head on my right side, my right arm under his neck with my left arm under his knees. He's mixed-heritage, with skin the colour of caramel and short, dark hair.

'This way: come with me,' says the police officer.

I run out of the front garden and turn right. Paul Brightley and another firefighter from Barking are with me but I'm ahead of them in the middle of the road. As I run I tilt my head down and continue to resuscitate the boy, his tiny bare chest rises as I blow into his mouth.

The police area car is around 50 yards from the house, and about halfway there, I lower my head to blow again into the boy's mouth while running. He exhales and vomits over my face. I look up briefly wipe my mouth on the sleeve of my fire tunic, but carry on running while blowing into his mouth. My face is covered in pungent acidic liquid. I think to myself, *He's just thrown up: good, he's breathing. Just got to get him into the car.* I continue blowing and think, *I'll do whatever it takes to save this boy's life.*

The police officer, who has left his colleague behind, opens the rear door on the near side of the area car. I get in and bundle the boy onto my lap. Paul gets in and sits to my right, and the Barking firefighter sits in the front as the constable starts the engine, taking-off like a fighter jet down the open end of Eton Road, sirens screaming. The constable picks up his radio handset.

'M-P, Juliet India-one. Active. Over!' The controller is in the Information Room at New Scotland Yard.

'Cars channel two, stand by. Juliet India-one, ahead. Over.'

'M-P Juliet India-one. En route Eton Road to King George V Hospital with an unconscious child on board. Running time approximately five to six, repeat: that's five to six minutes. Over.'

'Juliet India-one from M-P: all received…'

There's a pause. 'Juliet India-one. Are traffic escorting you. Over?'

'MP: negative.'

'Juliet India-one, there are two solos running from T-D-J.'

'MP: we haven't got time to wait.'

'Juliet India-one: understood. MP.'

'Cars stand by now… Tango Delta five… Tango Delta seven. CAD reference 10607: Juliet India-one to K-G-Five: running time five to six. That's five six now. Over.'

One of the two solos – police traffic bikes with a single officer/rider – responds.

'MP: Tango Delta seven. All received. We'll run to Eton Road and stand by there. Over.'

21.19 'Foxtrot four-two-two, from Station Officer McGuyver at 247 Eton Road. House of two floors, 6 by 10 metres, 25% of first floor alight. Ambulance reported delayed. Casualty removed by police vehicle with fire brigade crew resuscitating.'

Inside the police car I'm disoriented. Its low centre of gravity, unlike our machines, makes it stick hard to the road. As the car corners, its tyres screech into the night. I lean over the boy and continue to resuscitate him but the space is tight. He vomits again, this time it is much thicker, so I stick my first and index finger into his mouth and work them around to clear his airway before he vomits again, covering the middle of the back seat, and my fire tunic. It is impossible for me to make a seal over his mouth without ingesting the contents of the boy's stomach. I yank the fireproof neckerchief I'm wearing from under the collar of tunic and wipe the boy's mouth with it.

'Try the Respirex, Cliff,' says Paul. 'Here, mate: pass it to the leading hand.'

'The valve is open. I'll hold the cylinder – take the mask,' says the Barking firefighter.

I place the mask over the boy's mouth and squeeze the large plastic ball that pumps air into his lungs.

I look up and see that we are driving into the ambulance bay at King George V Hospital. I pick the boy up, step out of the car, and hang him upside down in the hope he's now breathing on his own and to drain and keep his airway open. *We've got him back. He's alive*, I say to myself. *Thank God he's alive.* I wedge two fingers on my right hand into the boy's mouth, press down on his tongue and run. His head is hanging down, his feet point skywards. I approach the accident unit, and see a sister in a dark-blue uniform, urging me towards her.

At this point I feel detached, emotionally and physically. It's as if I'm standing behind myself, watching as I run towards an unreal figure in a haunting scene.

I'm ghosting.

She's beckoning me as if in slow motion and pointing to where I should go. I run through the large double swing doors and am greeted by a buzz of raised but controlled voices – it's a jumble in my head. I'm surrounded by a medical team, like a bunch of angry wasps. I feel as though I'm watching over the entire scene from above. I hear a doctor shout, 'Where's the on-call paed? Have you – has anyone paged the duty paediatrician? We must have the consultant down here! Somebody bleep them urgently!' Her words ring through my head in a shattering tone.

'In there, mate: straight into resus,' a doctor says to me. The boy is laid out on a bed in the middle of the room. I'm standing level with his tiny waist. The middle of his chest is burnt. He appears unconscious, sleepy. A tangle of medical equipment flies around me, a young nurse stands on my left.

'I need to get a line in... got to... just got to get this in.'

I look at her. I look at the boy. 'OK, I'll help,' I say, and pick up his right arm and start to tap it in search of a vein in the crease of his forearm. 'Come on, come on, you little fucker!' I cry out in explosive desperation, willing him back, but the cannula on the tube won't go in, the vein is not strong enough and his life is ebbing away.

21:21 'Priority from Station Officer McGuyver. Ambulance still required, further casualty.'

Three minutes later Bill McGuyver sends another message requesting the attendance of the brigade photographer as he thinks this could be a fatal fire and evidence will then be recorded for a subsequent criminal investigation or inquest.

Radio messages are being transcribed, typed up and sent to the teleprinters at fire stations, bases and units all over the capital. Senior officers listening in on the radios in their cars hear the details of the fire by the control officers at Lambeth.

21:27 'Mobilising message: Oscar two-zero-two, media resources unit required. Four-pump fire. Persons reported: 247 Eton Road...'

Station Officer McGuyver is piecing together the details of what happened.

21:34 'One man escaped via internal staircase before arrival of brigade suffering from smoke inhalation and shock, awaiting removal. One woman, one boy escaped before arrival of brigade. Shocked, awaiting removal.'

ADO Boyes, Station Officer McGuyver, and the fire investigation team are looking around the front bedroom of the house, trying to establish the cause of the fire. There is no evidence to suggest arson.

In the resuscitation room activity slows down, the consultant in charge looks at the clock. I follow his eyes. I see the second hand freeze. I'm thinking and moving in slow motion, my entire body like a lead weight on a fishing line being dragged back against the tide. I'm rooted to the spot, standing by the boy's side. The doctor looks down from the clock and clears his throat.

'OK, everyone. That's it. Time of death is 21:34 hours.'

I'm paralysed. I look at the boy on the bed as thoughts go through my head.

He's not dead. He's alive. I know he is. He was breathing. I had him and he came back. He can't be dead.

One by one the medical team leave the resuscitation room. A nurse turns to me. She is wearing a green gown and she removes her opaque Latex gloves. 'Well done, mate. You gave it your best shot.'

'Gave it my best shot?' *He can't be dead I think. He CAN'T be. Why wasn't there an ambulance? Why have they stopped?*

Another nurse covers his body and walks out. I'm the last person to leave the cubicle as I look back at the tiny body of the young boy covered by a sheet.

Deputy Assistant Chief Officer Overall is the most senior officer on-call tonight in London.

21:43 'Echo two mobilised by pager at Orpington Fire Station...'

His seniority and experience are called on to deal with the unusual fire and because members of the brigade have moved the boy who escaped the fire along with his parents by ambulance. His 26 mile journey from Kent would normally take about an hour. Driving himself in an unmarked car on blue lights, he reaches the incident 38 minutes after his pager alert.

21:54 'Foxtrot two-zero-one. ADO Boyes. Stop. House of two floors 6m by 10m, 25% of first floor damaged by fire. Two hose reels, breathing apparatus. One boy rescued from first floor, via internal staircase by breathing apparatus crew, burned, overcome removed by police vehicle; one man, one woman, one boy escaped via internal staircase before arrival of brigade suffering from smoke inhalation and shock. Removed. All persons accounted for. Same as all calls.'

DACO Overall intercepts the message on the radio arriving at Eton Road at 22:21.

At the hospital, the consultant paediatrician interviews me and takes a statement. I have a chest X-ray as I have inhaled a lot of smoke, then I'm escorted to a claustrophobic waiting room where I sit down. The Barking firefighter is sitting on my left, Paul Brightley on my right. I'm unable to speak. I cannot take in the sheer scale of what is happening. We saved him. I saved him. He came back to life, but he's gone. Tears roll down my smoke-streamed face, my stinging eyes locked ahead.

I'm wearing my overtrousers and fire-boots. 'Come on, Cliff, don't cry. You'll start us all off,' says Paul. I sit in frustration, anger branded onto my skin. I'm struck by defeat and a massive sense of failure. I start to feel the enormity of what has happened as the loss begins to sink in.

An ambulance arrives at the hospital. Inside is Kim Hamilton, her partner Junior 'Reggie' Taylor, their five-year-old son, Karl. They are taken to another room and told by a doctor that their son has died.

His name is Gordon.

The family are kept separate from the three of us. I'm unable to comprehend what is happening. We get up and step out of the waiting room. An older woman arrives in a cab. She is Betty Hamilton, Kim's mother, who was at home in Upton Park Lane, Stratford, a few miles away when she was called and told her daughter's house was on fire. She is accompanied by her granddaughter Karlene.

We wait to be collected.

At 23:00, another senior officer, ADO O'Dwyer is mobilised. He comes to the hospital to collect Paul Brightley, the firefighter from Barking and myself in a brigade car. We walk silently through the doors to the car park. I look to my right and see Betty Hamilton standing, facing a wall of the hospital, crying. Alone in her grief, her head tilted down. A lump comes up in my throat and I fight hard to hold back the tears, but it is time to walk away. I feel isolated in my own grief, angry and helpless for a life I never knew, but was convinced that I had saved.

I don't know ADO O'Dwyer. He says nothing other than he will drop Paul and me at Ilford first. We drive to the station in complete silence. The radio is silent but for the occasional crack of static.

It is now one hour and 20 minutes after the initial call. Time has flown by.

23:22 'All gear made up.'

My machine, Foxtrot four-two-one, leaves the fire ground 'off-the-run': without its officer-in-charge. It arrives at Ilford at 23:26.

We reach the station and I go into the junior officers' room. I remove the vomit-stained fire tunic and place it in the dry-cleaning bag in the store next to the mess; I left the neckerchief in the back of the police car. I open my locker and find a spare. I go into the shower, I want to wash off every trace of this job but my mind is racing, going over events again and again, and all I can hear is the parents screaming. Then one of Ilford's firefighters who pokes his head around the door.

'Are you ready to put the ladder back on the run?' he says.

'No. I'm having a shower,' I reply.

'Cliff, it's the ladder. It should go back on the fucking run.'

'Why don't you fuck off? I'll put the ladder back on when I'm ready.'

'*You* fuck off – you arsehole!'

I feel like stepping from the shower and knocking him through the wall, such is the anger inside me.

Does anyone understand how I feel? Tricked and cheated, by what happened. *He was alive – Gordon. Yes, he was alive. I know he was. I had him, and he went. All that and he went. Why was there no ambulance? They'd have saved him. For fuck sake – he was only three and it's Christmas in five days.*

I step out of the shower. The firefighter who'd confronted me appears again.

'I'm sorry about that, Cliff. I just got carried away,' he says.

'Phone control and book us back on the run,' I reply.

It's now 21 December, just after midnight. Station Officer McGuyver picks up the phone. He calls the staff office at North East Area HQ in Stratford and dictates a 'tell the area commander message' outlining the incident. It will be relayed to Assistant Chief Officer Graham, who is in charge of the North East Area, who will see the message first thing in the morning. It is written down by the Station Officer in the staff office at Stratford. A few minutes later, the message is relayed back to the station over the teleprinter. I tear off the top copy and read it alone in the watch room. I am haunted by the words in that message covering the events of that night. Words that will torture me and which I'll go over and over several times a day, for a long time to come:

'Gordon Taylor, aged three, was rescued from the front bedroom on the first floor by breathing apparatus crews and was certified dead on arrival at King George's Hospital.'

He *wasn't* 'dead on arrival' at hospital. I didn't believe it. He was alive, and I had been subjected to the cruellest trick ever. The message is not true. I might not know it yet, but ahead of me lies more than a decade of soul-searching and questioning what happened that night.

I don't clearly remember what happened for the rest of that night. We didn't turn the wheel again; I just stayed on duty. With nine hours of the shift to go, confined to the station, it started to feel like a prison.

I lay on the fold-down bed in my room in darkness, not moving. I couldn't snap out of the detached feeling, my mind and body running through the reel of film of that night: backwards and forwards; reliving every second of the fire, the stench of vomit and the boy's pale, fading skin.

In the morning I was exhausted. It was too much but I

wanted answers. The Green Watch were subdued; everyone, everything felt distant but most of all I felt cheated.

We were approaching the end of our tour of duty. My next shift would be Christmas Day. I walked into the station office, sat at the typewriter and inserted some blank sheets from a memorandum pad, and started to tell the story of that fire in triplicate. It was copied to Station Officer McGuyver, also forwarded to the station commander; in turn it was forwarded to the area headquarters, with a copy placed on my personal file.

I hoped that completing the report, which became evidence in the brigade's investigation and for the coroner's hearing, would help me file the job away. When six bells sounded, I left the station, got into my car and headed towards Eton Road, following the route from the night before. I stopped at a florist's, one woman was talking to another who was behind the counter.

'Can I have a small bunch of those?' I pointed to some white flowers. The woman was oblivious to my anxiety, my stubble and my bloodshot, watery eyes.

'Of course you can. Are you alright?' asked the lady behind the counter.

'Not really. It's just...' My words faded and my eyes filled. I assumed that by now everyone in the local area knew what had happened. I felt as though everyone *should* know, but both women looked blank.

'It's for the little boy who died in that house fire last night.'

They don't know. They don't even care, I thought, but I wanted the whole world to know what happened to Gordon. I was convinced he was alive when we'd first arrived at the hospital. But he wasn't. The report said: 'Dead on arrival at King George's Hospital.'

I left the florist's, drove to the house and placed the flowers on the pavement outside 247 Eton Road. I stopped for a few minutes returned to my car and drove home, tears rolling down my cheeks.

CHAPTER 7

A Tunnel

I owned an abridged version of the Gideon Bible that we were given during our first week at training school. I kept it in my fire-station locker. I also kept a large, thick children's picture-book Bible at home, with the most amazing colourful painted images, which I'd had since I was about nine years old. Every time I stay in a hotel, I always check the drawers by the room's bed for a Gideon Bible. Although I'm not really that spiritual, I simply find its presence reassuring.

I arrived at my basement flat on the morning after the fire in which Gordon died. I had four days leave ahead of me, but everything was starting to blur into shades of grey, with a constant foul-smelling mist surrounding me: the stench of death. The Green Watch were due to start our new tour of duty on Christmas Day. I felt completely empty but I wanted to talk about what happened to Gordon; to whom, I didn't know. I was like a repeatedly flipping coin – landing one side on rage, the other on upset as I desperately tried to hold things together.

On Monday 23 December, I drove to Smithfield meat market in the City of London – adjacent to the Charterhouse Street cold store where I'd been to a 15-pump fire two years before. That evening I wrote in my diary: 'Went and got the turkey for Mum and Dad after a sleepless night... got to bed again at 1am.' The noise and the bustle of the Christmas market was a welcome distraction, it overrode the booming rage in my mind. The lack of sleep was affecting me physically. I couldn't concentrate and wasn't eating. From Tuesday 24 December until the following Tuesday 31 December, my diary was blank, I always kept at least a basic record of each day but I was slipping away from the real world and felt the lead weight tugging me down.

Consumed by grief and a growing need to find out what happened to the victims I encountered in my work, I decided to visit Gordon's parents. Kim Taylor and her partner, Reggie, who were staying in a council high rise in Plaistow a few days later. The flat was bare, and their other children weren't there. They seemed pleased to see me, and welcomed me into their home.

I knocked on the door. A woman answered.

'Hello. I'm Leading Firefighter Thompson... Clifford.'

'Come in,' said Kim. 'Come in, we... I mean me and Reggie, we're so grateful for everything you did.'

Reggie looked at me, his eyes burning white-hot and bloodshot. Tears rolled down his face.

'Would you like a cup of tea?' Kim asked.

'No, thank you,' I replied.

'I can't understand. They say Gordon.... Gordon vomit in your arms. I can't understand why?'

I tried to calm Reggie down, telling him that Gordon was now at rest, but I felt like an intruder on the family's grief. I felt a sense of duty towards Kim and Reggie, but at the same time, felt powerless through grief. I wasn't sure if I was trying to help them, or myself.

'Thank you, Clifford. So much, man. You try to save G's life. The Lord has taken him. He's in heaven now. Bless you, Clifford, for all you do.'

I nodded. The reel of film that was my perspective of events had slowed to a frame-by-frame pace. But I felt comforted now. Some of the Green Watch would have thought I was mad: their way of dealing with such a terrible fire was to shut it out because the next one could happen at any time. But I felt compelled to seek some understanding.

The meeting with Kim and Reggie was brief. I looked at them in the eye of the storm that was their loss, and considered how fortunate I was. But I couldn't let go of what had happened. I felt guilty that I'd lost their son. Before leaving I promised them I'd go to Gordon's funeral. I felt that making contact would give me answers. I was the last person to see Gordon alive, and as such had to see it through. I thought going to the funeral would help me, but I doubted that any of my Green Watch colleagues would want to come. Everyone deals with a loss in their own way and I respected their choice.

I felt as if I was still crawling slowly along a narrow tunnel, trying to get away from the fire that killed Gordon, and was beginning to wonder if I'd ever recover from what happened that night.

The weeks just before the Eton Road fire had been difficult for me. One night we were called to a collision between a car and a pedestrian on the edge of Leytonstone's ground. I was in charge of Ilford's pump ladder. When we arrived, Leytonstone's pump and the rescue tender from East Ham were already on the scene, its crew wedging large blocks into both sides of the car to stabilise it. A man was freed from underneath it and the paramedics started chest compressions. I shouted at people spilling into the busy road to get back, and even with my experience, was amazed by how people stopped to look as the paramedics ripped open his shirt and pushed down on his chest.

It looked as if the man wasn't going to make it, and seeing someone clinging to life was worse than coming across a stiff. The next day I wrote in my diary that I'd been, 'tossing and turning all night', and a few days later I felt, 'under a lot of strain'. On a day off, I phoned Wanstead police station to find out how the man was. The officer said the 71-year-old had been to his bridge club. Walking home alone, he had stepped into the road to cross but looked the wrong way. He was run over by a car that continued, then hit by a second that trapped him. He died later at hospital.

The old man's death had quite an impact on me. It made me think about the fragility of life, and how quickly it can come to an end. It unsettled me. But it was nothing compared to what was to come a few weeks later at Eton Road.

I reported for work at 9am on Christmas Day, in charge of the pump ladder, and second-in-command of the watch. It's usually a relaxed and informal day. The officers swapped roles with some of the watch members. The station officer would be the duty man, the sub does the cooking and the junior buck is allowed to sit in the front of the machine in the governor's place on emergency calls. Stand-down routines operate in the period between Christmas Day and New Year's day, so the watch only attended emergency calls, and completed the basic routines necessary to maintain safety: testing breathing apparatus sets and checking the machines were operationally ready.

Watch members played pool or snooker, cards and board games and read or watched television. We pretended to keep up the traditions we'd inherited, but this was a Christmas Day like no other in my life.

A Tunnel

There was a strained atmosphere. Gordon's death had cut through the watch. I was feeling so much anger and loss. After our Christmas lunch I started a food fight, another bizarre tradition that happened on some fire stations, even though horseplay was banned. I was trying to break the tension, keeping at the forefront of my mind the spirit of firefighters who just carried on with the job no matter how tough things were.

I threw a handful of sherry trifle across the mess then planted a giant handful on to Frankie's bald head. He squared up to me. 'Cliff, you fucking idiot!'

'Fuck off!' I replied.

'I'm gonna have you. Outside the station. I'm going to kill you!'

'I'm warning you: I'll have you on a charge,' I said, the tension rising.

'Fuck you!' he replied.

I turned and walked away and the Green Watch dispersed to different parts of the station, as we tried to escape each other's company. No one was talking. When we were dismissed at six, I drove to my parents' house for a late Christmas dinner, although any sense of celebration was lost on me. The cracks were widening, the strain growing and the armour plating was beginning to buckle.

I worked on Boxing Day, and decided I was definitely going to Gordon's funeral on New Year's Eve. Then, before our first night shift, I called in sick 'with flu-like symptoms'. I had spent the previous evenings at home, alone and without the company of a girlfriend. I couldn't concentrate, and I kept watching a video of a Miles Davis concert that I recorded on Christmas Eve. I hoped the music would distract me, but I was overtired, yet unable to sleep for more than a couple of hours, my mood flicking between anger and despair. I felt cheated and that is what shook me the most. I tried listening to loud music, I screamed down the phone at my mates – aggression and grief a potent cocktail that was corroding my soul. I was being provocative: I wanted everyone to know what had happened to Gordon, and if they didn't understand, I hoped they'd at least feel sorry for me. I just couldn't understand why a young life was lost, especially so close to Christmas – a time of birth and celebration.

I felt sad and ashamed at losing Gordon. Although his death wasn't my fault, I blamed myself. I'd lost grasp of reality and in its place was a deep sense of failure. But I couldn't express to anyone what it was like to feel his life ebbing away. No one seemed interested, and even those who expressed their concern in the days following the tragedy seemed to assume that life went on. As professional firefighters, we weren't expected to show our feelings; it was just our job. I ghosted through the days and nights, reliving every moment of that fire. I felt that Gordon had taken my courage with him, leaving me defenceless and vulnerable.

I hoped that maybe some good would come from his death. I imagined myself getting a medal for bravery – except Gordon had died. Who would decorate a failure? I felt all the responsibility for his loss, a sequence of events that had conspired against me in the most extraordinary way. But it was the association of the death of a child at Christmas that troubled me the most. Why? How could a life end before it started? Why was I so convinced that I had saved Gordon? I knew that Gordon was alive: in the house, in my arms, in the police car. I refused to believe he was already dead by the time we'd reached the hospital. I was the person clinging on to him in those final moments. I felt the fluttering pulse. He did look sleepy, but he was not dead. I went over and over the scenario in my mind, every background noise in my deadened state, shattered by Kim and Reggie's screams. I remembered the haunting image of Gordon's grandmother, Betty, looking down at the ground outside the hospital, in solitary grief. I had seen her, but left her and walked away, all the while thinking to myself over and over: *Why*?

I was exhausted, but determined to go to the funeral, thinking it would help me put things to rest. I wanted to get back to my old self, and to work.

One evening just before the funeral, I pulled my heavy children's Bible from the bookcase. The pictures looked so bright in my numbness, and as I flicked through the pages I felt myself slowly rising in the same way that I had at the funeral of Colin Townsley after the King's Cross fire. Something was calling me, the words were speaking to me: All these things I will give you, if you fall down and worship me.

I was 25. I had my whole life and career ahead of me. Dreams of being in charge of my own watch. Maybe one day making it to divisional officer, and I'd be the one in charge of a 10-pumper driving my own car with a magnetic blue light, men and women would look to me as their leader. I had been riding high, tipped for great things, but what happened to Gordon floored me – it was instantaneous. It's common among emergency-service workers to have one or two incidents that stay with them, no matter their experience. And this, I was to realise, caused a permanent change in me.

My parents were concerned. I lived by myself so they could only keep a check on me from a distance. I was irrational, temperamental and cruising out of control. They knew I wasn't myself and, one night, when they thought I'd reached crisis point, took me to accident and emergency at the Royal

London Hospital in Whitechapel. It was a simple consultation with the on-call psychiatrist. We sat in a room and I poured my heart out, crying, repeatedly asking him, 'Why?' He nodded as he listened. I remember vividly holding out my hand, which he held. I felt a surge like 50,000 volts running through me, which, just maybe, was the slow start of me getting my life back on track.

The psychiatrist at the hospital referred me to Professor Colin Murray Parkes, a consultant psychiatrist and one of the world's leading authorities on grief. I had no idea I was heading for such capable hands.

In the meantime, I continued to stay with my parents.

One night, I was resting on the bed trying to sleep and I began feeling an amazing sense of spirituality that I had never before known, as if I were being pulled or urged up. It was Sunday 29 January, and in my numb state, I got up from the sofa-bed and told my father I was going out. I walked the long road towards the Underground station and into the Redbridge United Reformed Church. I had never spontaneously walked into a church before; I'd only ever gone to pre-arranged services, like a wedding. But I felt it could make me feel better, that I need to look for a way to help myself and that going to church would be a good place to start.

There were about 20 people in the congregation in the simple wood-panelled 1950s church that looked like a community centre. I had no idea what I was going to do, but I felt calm for the first time in nine days. The vicar beckoned me to the front, where I joined a queue and knelt at the altar taking my first Holy Communion. He had a friendly, wise face with a short beard and grey hair. He introduced himself after the service.

'Hello. I'm Mervyn Popplestone. What brings you here

today?'

'I don't know. It's... I've had a terrible experience: the loss of a child. Well... I'm a firefighter, and this small boy, Gordon, he died in my arms. In Ilford, near here. We rescued him, I just don't know...'

'It's OK, rest and I'll pray for you.'

I felt calmer, and wondered if he could give me the answers and clear a way through the tunnel. I felt Gordon's aura; was it fate that I was meant to hold him in my arms as his soul slipped away?

'Can I come back another time and see you?' I asked.

'Of course.'

'It's just, I'd like to go to the funeral...'

'Come back any time, Clifford. You are welcome.'

The next day I returned to the church, and knocked on Father Popplestone's door at the vicarage.

'Clifford. Welcome. Come in. How are you?'

'Well, I'm better, but still very upset. I'm determined to go to the funeral. It's tomorrow – New Year's Eve.'

'Would you like me to pray for you?'

'Yes. Please. I've got these fire-brigade cap badges for the other children...'

'I'll bless them for you,' he replied. 'What would you like me to do for you?' He was sitting at a dark wood antique bureau, like a writing table.

'I just wish there was a way of understanding it all: some way of being able to reflect and make sense of life. A way of finding an answer.'

'It's very difficult for us to answer the question "why?", Clifford. Leave me your address. I promise I'll send you something.'

The funeral was the next day, the last of 1991. I wasn't really up to driving, so my father gave me a lift to Ilford. The Blue Watch were on their first day shift. I didn't see any of my own watch, who were due to return in a few days.

For the second time in my career, I opened my locker and took out the sombre, parade dress worn to a funeral: highly-polished shoes, traditional wool tunic and flat cap and blue-black trousers and a thick webbing belt coated in polish until it glistened. I pushed the peak of the cap down firmly over my eyes. The uniform comforted me, and I began to feel strong again.

I was still exhausted but determined to get through the day for Gordon, and his family, then Doreen arrived at the fire station. She was a local police officer who was a friend of the Green Watch. She visited the station regularly and we often worked with her at jobs. She heard about the fatal fire and came to see us on Boxing Day. She offered to take me to the funeral, which was taking place at the cemetery in St Patrick's in Leytonstone. We didn't say much and I was disappointed that none of my Green Watch mates wanted to come, but it was Christmas, nearly the start of 1992, and many of them had children. Maybe they would have found it too upsetting. Doreen took a keen interest in the community where she served, although I have no recollection of her being at Eton Road on the night of the fire.

We arrived at the cemetery early, then as the cortege arrived, I stood to attention and saluted as the hearse containing Gordon's tiny coffin passed me. Kim and Betty looked and smiled at me, surprised but pleased to see I was there. I walked behind the cortege and after a short service in the chapel, we gathered around the grave in which Gordon was to be buried. As his coffin was lowered, Kim and Reggie stood over Gordon, as I shovelled some earth on to his plot. Then the family gathered and placed flowers on top.

I felt incredibly proud to be there, representing the brigade and all the firefighters, and knew I had to stay calm.

Kim and Betty asked me back in one of the funeral cars to Betty's house in Upton Park.

'It would mean so much to us,' said Kim.

'Of course,' I replied. Doreen decided to go home so I jumped into the large black Rolls Royce and sat in silence until we reached her house in Upton Park Lane.

I met the whole family, including Kim's sister, and I played with Karlene and Karl. Around five that evening I decided to leave. I said goodbye and walked for a bit onto Green Street, then towards Romford Road. As I reached the junction by the police station I turned right but it would take ages to walk the few miles to Ilford. I paused for a moment and a car passed. It sounded its horn and the driver waved at me. Then another and another. Then it dawned on me that the drivers thought I was off to a New Year's Eve fancy dress party, wearing Edwardian fire rig. I knew it was only a misunderstanding, but it felt cruel. I flagged down a police patrol car and persuaded the officer to give me a lift back to Ilford.

At the station, I changed and went to my parents' house, then all I remember was going to my flat in Bow just before midnight. I think I took a cab – I'm left with large gaps in time that I can't account for. I turned on the radio in my basement flat, tuned it to BBC Radio 4 and waited in silence for the sound of Big Ben's chimes on the radio.

At midnight I counted each ring in my head: one, two, three, four, five, six, seven, eight, nine, 10, 11... on the stroke of 12, I paused and let out a sigh as the sound of *Auld Lang Syne* was played my face shimmering with fresh tears.

It was the end of 1991, and now, I thought, I could let go of Gordon. Although I didn't know it, I was also about to let go of the career I loved. I was in pieces, crawling slowly along a tunnel with only a dim light in the distance. I felt like a failure, not the hero I'd wanted to be.

PART TWO: Ten Days
New York, February 1993

Fear, tenderness – these emotions were so despised
that they could be admitted into consciousness
only at the cost of redefining what it meant to be a man

from Regeneration, by Pat Barker

CHAPTER 8

Marshals

We reached the police line at about half past six in the evening. There were barriers everywhere. I pleaded with a cop. 'Look, officer, we're from the UK, we're filming with the fire marshals. I can see John Stickevers, their boss at the command post over there... Please let us past the line.'

'Stay there, sir,' the officer replied.

We were standing on West Street looking at a bridge over the road in front of us, just beyond it we could see the base of the North Tower of the World Trade Center, and further along the Vista International Hotel. There were flags hanging limply over its entrance, where the emergency service workers were mostly concentrated.

The Fire Department of New York (FDNY) control unit was parked outside the hotel, and there were scores of vehicles from all the emergency services, along with crowds of onlookers. We couldn't see any casualties being helped from the building; the street was full of ambulances as we filmed the scene.

It was 26 February 1993. Earlier that day a bomb was detonated in a basement car park in one of the towers. I had arrived in New York City just a few days before, my life now barely recognisable from how it had been before. In less than a year, I had left the LFB and had embarked on a new life and career, working in television production. Now here I was, documenting a disaster when, previously, I would have been at its centre.

I had my first meeting with Professor Colin Murray-Parkes, the consultant psychiatrist at the Royal London Hospital to whom I'd been referred, in early 1992. I was struck by his calming presence at the first consultation. He was in his mid-60s, and patiently listened to me and helped make sense of the disasters I had encountered. He was interested in the idea that firefighters were suddenly thrown into dramatic and demanding events without any warning, and often in the middle of the night, having been woken up. This contrasted with a soldier being sent to war, who has time to prepare psychologically. He built up a detailed picture of my background, observing that I'd 'coped well with the rigours of being a fireman' and had 'considerable potential'. But he also thought the accumulated experience of stressful emergencies left me vulnerable. He diagnosed me with post-traumatic stress disorder.

Post-traumatic stress disorder (PTSD) wasn't a new condition. Soldiers coming back from World War I were diagnosed with what was then known as shell shock, and it's thought that the term was first used in the 1970s to describe many symptoms displayed by veterans returning from the Vietnam War. It affects sufferers in several different ways, including flashbacks, feeling irritable and guilty about being involved in and surviving a traumatic event. It's only now, looking back, that I realise how unwell I was.

The worst symptom I experienced was withdrawal. After a month's sick leave I was put on light duties at the area HQ behind Stratford Fire Station on a desk job. At first it was a welcome distraction from the tragedy I'd been part of. My job involved inputting data about fires into a computer, in an office with civilians, most of them admin workers. It was also where the senior officers were based. There were no emergencies, no drills and much less banter compared to a fire station.

I was away from my watch colleagues at Ilford, and even when my former Red Watch colleagues were on-duty at Stratford Fire Station just across the yard, I avoided them.

I bumped into a mate from Leytonstone in the yard at Stratford one day, who said he'd heard about me putting on my parade uniform on New Year's Eve for the funeral. Word had got around the neighbouring stations, and the pride I'd felt going to Gordon's funeral was replaced by a sense of shame now. I'd felt I'd had to pay my respects, but maybe at the same time I'd been too immersed. I felt an incredible sense of failure, thinking that Gordon's death was my responsibility. I still went over and over the events, and dreamed about it every night. I felt detached from everything around me, compounded by the fact that I was living alone and not in a relationship.

I had become more cautious – a symptom that has stayed with me to this day. Gone was my ability to make a snap decision, when I used to be able make life-and-death decisions, such as ordering a crew into a burning building. Now I often think through every conceivable scenario about the simplest of tasks – whether to go shopping, or go for a day out just to have fun. My mind goes back and forth over all the possible outcomes, including what could go wrong, which means I spend so long deciding what to do, I can often end up with no time to do it.

Another symptom I experienced was anger, shouting at people and getting into rows. I'd criticise friends who were drinking heavily, even though I'd gone through phases of drinking a lot myself. I either fell out with other friends because of my attitude or felt unable to talk to those that I remained close to. I'd kept in touch with Amy, my on-and-off ex-girlfriend, but our relationship became another victim of my turbulent state of mind and I lost a great friend.

I found forming close relationships difficult. I couldn't make a commitment before the death of Gordon, but now it was impossible. I couldn't settle; I'd just go on a few dates then give up. Somehow being a 'former' firefighter had none of the appeal, and I couldn't face going over my history. I'd always thought I'd get married in my mid- to late 20s. I wanted to be settled but it felt hard to explain the gaps in my life and I still couldn't fully open up and talk about Gordon's death without getting upset, I existed in a state of subdued isolation.

I was constantly on edge – another classic symptom. The slightest loud bang, even a door shutting, would make me jump. I was living alone and working in an office with people I didn't know. I had sunk to my lowest point and with no way up. The majority of my close friends stopped asking how I was. I felt locked in with my own anxieties, fears and depression.

I stayed on light duties until August 1992, when the LFB's occupational health doctor, based on the advice of Dr Parkes, decided that there was no guarantee of my symptoms not escalating again. I was declared 'permanently unfit for duty'. I was 25 years old.

When it came to clearing out my locker, I could barely look my Green Watch colleagues in the eye. That was the worst time. I'd carved a character for myself for seven years; now I was no one. I was soon to be an outsider. I didn't have a leaving function or party. I felt my career had been cut too short for that, and felt embarrassed 'celebrating' my seven years. But the officers and the civilian staff at Area HQ presented me with a tankard on my last day. I wanted to disappear, become anonymous – just be a nobody. I was ghosting again. The largest part of what had defined me for so many years had gone, leaving a void, and I was heartbroken.

It would be many years until I could look back and understand that I had become strained by so many terrible experiences from an extremely young age. I was 18 when I joined the fire service, just 19 on my first posting to Stratford. Although I didn't go to the King's Cross fire, it had taken its toll on me as I imagined the horror of that night, and just how much worse it must have been for those firefighters who had attended, and for the victims and their families. Perhaps I'd grown up too fast and just seen too much.

Attitudes to disaster victims gradually changed. Following King's Cross, Dr James Thompson, a psychologist from University College London, began to lead the way with research and the term PTSD appeared more in the media. In an attitude that has gone full circle, he conceded in 2009 that PTSD was now being diagnosed 'too liberally' for things such as 'bullying and minor collisions on the road'.

The 1980s was a time of many terrible disasters played out to the public by the news media, including the Bradford City football stadium fire, the Hillsborough disaster, the sinking of the Herald of Free Enterprise, the Lockerbie PanAm crash, the Kegworth air crash, the sinking of the Marchioness pleasure boat. I'd been on duty that night and remember helping the staff officers throw lifejackets from the stores at Stratford into the back of the divisional van. The driver – a firefighter had a look of terror on his face as he headed for central London and the River Thames. Sadly 51 poor souls perished that night. These were just a few of the terrible tragedies from a single decade, but each one helped to raise awareness of

PTSD. By the time I left the fire service more emergency service workers were being diagnosed with PTSD. I personally knew of two.

Maybe in my case the events that I assumed were being filed neatly away were quietly damaging my mind, eroding some psychological 'wiring' that would eventually lead to symptoms flaring up. Maybe I was emotionally flawed. As I got older my ability to bounce back lessened. Just being in a state of readiness or 'high alert' was in itself stressful. I continued to work on this area in therapy long after the 1990s, and even today I get run-down easily, spending days recovering from what feels like a semi-permanent state of exhaustion. How could it be that some firefighters survive 30 years doing the job without suffering PTSD? It didn't make any sense. Even now this is something I've struggled to come to terms with: the notion that somehow I was weak, or flawed – and this still troubles me. I'm also a light sleeper and am woken by the slightest noise – another damaging symptom.

I continued to meet Professor Parkes every month or so until the summer of 1993. He suggested I consider a change of career, telling me I was hard-working and committed – he said he wished some of his medical students were as dedicated as me. It felt like a pivotal moment, because he didn't judge me. His faith in my abilities strengthened my own belief. He understood me. He was patient and sympathetic.

I stopped seeing Professor Parkes when he retired in 1993 and was moved to another psychiatrist's list. It was hard being unemployed with no career, and I felt a real sense of panic about my future. It was then that I began to feel I'd have to pull myself up. There was no magic cure for the guilt, shame and anxiety I felt.

I'd always seen myself as a practical person, a worker, not particularly academic. But one of the ways I learned to cope with my job as a firefighter was through studying. In September 1991, just before Gordon's death, I signed up for a degree in humanities at Birkbeck, part of the University of London, learning everything across the spectrum, including film theory, media studies and American geography and history. I met new people and found that as my knowledge increased, it bolstered my personal life, and eventually my career – although it would be many years before I'd feel the benefits of this. Crucially, it was a key to a new future, and a reprogrammed 'me'. That first year at university was hard, but it also helped me to come to terms with leaving the fire service.

In September 1992 I started a new academic year. I had just scraped through my first with an average score, but was starting to feel a small change for the better. That autumn, I worked as a volunteer on a student film. It was only for a couple of weeks, but it put some structure and direction back into my life. I was offered the role of runner, but by the afternoon of the first day I had been promoted to production manager, troubleshooting issues that came up from hiring equipment to booking location catering. I enjoyed it, but quickly discovered that film-making was more collaborative and consultative in comparison to firefighting; I was frustrated by the lack of discipline, with schedules constantly over-running, and I struggled to adopt a more diplomatic tone. I was thinking and acting as I had in my previous career, where a strict hierarchy was adhered to. Change was happening, but in very small steps.

As my interest in the media and film-making grew, I thought

about becoming a television researcher. I wanted to work on documentaries but the prospect of being a journalist seemed well out of my reach. Yet the Victorian founder of 'modern' firefighting, Eyre Massey Shaw, laid out strict criteria for firefighters, one of which was to have an enquiring mind. I believed this, at least, would help me in pursuit of my new career. A previous encounter with a TV producer set me on the right path.

In 1990, while at Kingsland, a film crew had followed some of the watches for a documentary called *Fire!* for the ITV London broadcaster, Thames Television. Keen to learn more about the production process, I'd chatted to the producer and got back in touch with him after I left the brigade. I was fascinated by a book I'd read about New York City's armed fire marshals by New York-based psychologist Peter Micheels called *Heat: The Fire Investigators and Their War on Arson and Murder*, and was intrigued by their stories about murders, insurance fraud and revenge fires. I thought it would make a good subject for a documentary. My producer contact agreed, and suggested I spend a couple of days working up my idea in his North London office, so I sent a request to the New York Fire Department (FDNY) for permission to film. A week or so later, the fire department replied to my request and were happy for filming to go ahead. I hadn't pitched the idea to a broadcaster, but decided to go ahead with the filming 'on spec', as a pilot or taster, and shoot on a shoestring budget, with semi-professional equipment.

With less than a year's experience, I'd landed a significant assignment – although I knew I still had a long way to go in order for it to become a broadcast documentary. But I had this one great idea and didn't want to let go of it. I'd clinched the deal because I'd been a firefighter, and now for the first time since Gordon's death, I felt I could make use of some of the experience I'd gained.

The New York Fire Department is the second-largest fire service in the world; London is the third. I'd had the pleasure of spending some time with my American counterparts in June 1991, when I went on holiday to New York for the first time. As with everything in New York, the scale was massive: tall buildings, larger fire trucks. I'd arranged to visit two fire-houses while I was there, and had lunch with one of the crews. We had a laugh and exchanged some badges – I even rode with them to what turned out to be a false alarm. The front-line firefighter in New York seemed to work to very specific functions. If one was deployed to take the fire extinguisher into a burning building, then that's what they did. With so many tall buildings and skyscrapers, the FDNY also had regular experience of working high above ground.

But the marshals in particular fascinated me. Although they work for the Bureau of Fire Investigation, which is part of the fire department, they are firefighters who train as arson investigators. So they attend fires, wear the helmet, tunic and boots of firefighters. But they are different: they carry hand-cuffs, a warrant card embossed with a gold shield, and have exactly the same powers of arrest as the police. At that time, they also carried a .357 calibre Smith & Wesson revolver.

The New York Fire Department had a dedicated team of arson investigators at three bases across the city – nothing like London, which only ever had a handful of fire-investigation teams on duty at any one time, and they didn't have the police powers that the marshals did.

Now here I was, standing just feet away from a bomb site, trying to get some shots. I was working with a camerawoman,

Hester, who I'd met on the student film. We went out a few times and became good friends.

We'd arrived in the city three days earlier, when we'd gone to see John Stickevers, chief of the Bureau of Fire Investigation, who introduced us to his staff officer, Ed. The chief asked about our plans, made us sign an indemnity form so we could ride with the marshals, and then we were driven to one of the bases in the Bronx in a distinctive blue Lincoln Continental car.

The chief said it would be too dangerous to travel with our camera equipment to the Bronx on public transport so we were escorted to their base a few miles north of Brooklyn. It was in an old firehouse, and we were introduced to the 'boss', Don Forster. He showed us around – there was a large but bare office. None of the desks matched and there were hundreds of beige files perilously stacked up on them next to manual typewriters. He introduced us to the marshals on duty and arranged for us to be collected on the days that we planned to film. Don drew up a rota in the diary. We had just over a week ahead of us.

At the bombed towers, fire trucks were still arriving, by now coming from all of the city's five boroughs. It was a freezing-cold night, and outside the cordon there were dozens of ambulances and police cars parked in grey icy slush. Then a cop moved the barrier where we were standing to one side to allow a Con Edison power truck towing a generator into the disaster zone. Temporary payphones built into a trailer had been towed just inside the cordon. All three were in use by people, one wearing a hard hat, but none were facing into the booth concentrating on their calls, all were looking down West Street towards the North Tower. We were so close to the base of the tower, it was impossible to see all the way up it, and it was raining – heavy, chilled droplets adding to the chaos and misery.

I looked to my right and saw a blue Lincoln Continental car approach the barrier. 'Hester – that car, it looks like it's one of the marshals.' She lowered the camera and caught up with me as I ran towards the car. I've got nothing to lose, I thought and I waved my arms to attract the driver's attention. He lowered the window. I hoped it would be one of the marshals we knew, but I didn't recognise the detective, who was alone and wearing an overcoat, smart shirt and tie.

'Excuse me, sir. Are you a fire marshal? We need your help.'

'Yes, I am. What's the problem?' he asked.

'My name is Cliff Thompson. This is my camerawoman, Hester. We're filming with some of your colleagues at the Bronx base—'

He interrupted. 'But I'm at the Brooklyn base and I don't know anything about this.'

'I wonder if you could help. We're supposed to be filming with your colleagues tonight – we have permission from Chief Stickevers, I'm sure he's here—'

He interrupted again. 'Jump in the car. I'll take you through the cordon.'

We bundled our bags and the camera into the back of the Lincoln, and he drove forward a short distance. As a cop approached the car, the marshal lowered his window and thrust his badge up at him.

'OK, buddy. I'm from the BFI and these guys are with me,' the marshal said as he raised his shield towards the cop, and without another word the wooden barrier was moved to one side and Hester and I were inside the cordon.

The marshal drove the three of us under the bridge, and

after about a 100 yards stopped outside the entrance to the Vista International, where the fire department's command post was located.

I immediately spotted John Stickevers, who was a big man with a rusty-coloured beard and hair. He looked like a cowboy who'd stumbled into Manhattan straight from a western. He was standing with his staff officer, Ed. A tall man probably of Italian origin with a broad New York accent, Ed was wearing the standard detective outfit of suit covered by a beige trench coat. He was carrying a large portable cellular telephone with a battery that was about the same size as one fitted to a car.

I walked over and we shook hands. 'Evening, John.'

'Hey, hello Clifford. This is pretty big. What do you think?'

'I've never seen anything like it in my career.'

'It's enormous. Would you like to go down and film in the basement?'

'Us go down there? Of course – that would be fantastic.' I couldn't believe what I was hearing, I looked at Hester. We both started fumbling with the kit.

'Great. Ed will take you down with a couple of the marshals – Jon and Mike. Just one thing Clifford: the FBI are all over this; it's a major crime scene. They're watching everyone going in and out. You are the only film crew that will be allowed down there tonight. Understand?'

'John – Ed, thanks so much. I can't believe it—'

'Just one condition,' he interrupted. 'You can film what you want, but if we see any of your pictures on tomorrow's news... Well, let's say you probably won't ever be visiting the United States again. Just sit on it for a bit. Is that a deal?' he asked.

'That's fine. Thank you so much.'

It was less than a year since I'd left the London Fire Brigade.

A major disaster had struck again, and I was about to be taken to its very heart.

Hester and I waited outside the entrance, which was close to the hotel. We were standing just inside a pair of fire doors that normally served only as a fire exit. The lights were on, and there was a long line of hose snaking down the stairwell. The impromptu entrance led to some tatty wooden stairs and it was clear this was not a route intended to be used by the public – even in normal circumstances.

As we waited, Hester was adjusting the settings on the camera, while I checked the connections from the battery pack to a handheld light. There was a lot of shouting. One of the marshals, Jon, walked past us. The other marshal, Mike, was behind us.

'Mike, are you gonna take them in?' said Jon, then he turned around and nodded to someone outside. Ed pushed his way through, and the Brooklyn marshal who had picked us up walked into the entrance and stood next to me.

'This is my man, Clifford,' said Ed to the group. 'Hey Jon! Wait at the bottom of the stairs.'

It was an extraordinary scene: Ed and the Brooklyn marshal in their overcoats, Mike and Jon wearing their fire-rig; Mike had a large white badge on his helmet with the words 'Supervising Fire Marshal'. I hadn't seen any casualties and no bodies were being removed. The atmosphere was quite relaxed for a major incident that had started about six hours earlier.

We walked forwards as a group as we made our descent into the North Tower. There was no damage in the stairwell, where the walls were painted yellow and lit by harsh fluorescent lights. At the bottom of a few flights of stairs we reached a door with a cable hanging above our heads. 'Watch your head, watch your head,' repeated Ed as we passed through. We were now in a much wider and higher corridor, which looked as if it was meant to be used by the buildings maintenance workers. I could see the first real signs of damage. Jon and Ed were in front.

'You gotta watch out: there's a lot of rubble here. There's broken glass and it's very slippery,' said Ed, without looking round at me. Mike walked in front of us as Hester filmed from behind.

After a few seconds we passed through a set of double doors that connected the corridor to the car park, where it was total darkness. Voices echoed and the sound of messages crackled from a police radio. There were two cops standing inside the doors, who looked unconcerned at our arrival. Jon and Mike had been down to the basement several times already. The marshals turned on their flashlights, I turned on the camera light and in front of us was a shell of a car – no wheels, windows or seats just an ash-coloured burnt-out wreck.

The whole floor had collapsed so we were now standing a considerable way below where the floor should have been. There was a tangle of metal rods that were part of the floor's reinforcement, collapsed slabs, conduit pipes for electricity cables, and in the middle of the car park, a large hole in the floor and in the ceiling above us, another large hole about 60ft wide and 80ft across, exposing the floor of basement level one. The opening in the level we were standing on dropped down into an abyss a couple of 100 feet below us. We couldn't get anywhere close to this hole in the floor as it was blocked with cars and rubble and sloped steeply toward the exposed floors beneath.

We were standing in the second basement level at the epicentre of the explosion. What little light there was in the

North Tower was passing through four giant holes directly underneath it. The floors of basement levels one and two had been blown open, and debris cascaded like a rocky waterfall down through the existing openings of levels three and four. Debris dropped to level five and the shock wave caused pipes to burst, damaging the entire subterranean infrastructure, six levels under the tower. It also caused damage to the Port Authority Trans Hudson rail tunnels that passed close to the bottom of level six.

Ed shone his flashlight at the ramp on the far side of the building, but it was too dark and too distant for us to see clearly, apart from what looked like a large opening on the opposite side of the building, which was the ramp where cars would enter from the level above. A Jeep had been blown sideways across the car park, wiping out another car. I had never seen such damage in my life, and at that moment I felt the same detachment and disorientation I had known earlier in my career as a firefighter. It was impossible to take in the scene but unlike the previous disasters, my role now was just as an observer, and an outsider. Because I was no longer a firefighter, I could concentrate for the first time on putting the pieces of the jigsaw together. I'd travelled 3,000 miles to film the marshals and somehow found myself in the middle of a disaster that was being reported by the media all over the world.

I was back inside the triangle of fire.

I turned to Ed on my right, who moved half left so we could just see each other's eyes in the flashlight's glow. Hester panned the camera to her left, catching Ed in the right of the frame. The tape was rolling.

'What actually happened here, Ed?' I asked.

'We can't say right now.' His reply was guarded. There was

a pause then he moved closer to me, looking shaken but angry. 'You will probably be part of history standing here. This is devastation beyond belief. Unbelievable – you can't imagine. This is the city of New York – it's not a third-world country and we're not at war with anybody.'

His reply, full of anger and emotion shook me; the light I was holding reflected off the broad lenses of his glasses, and I seized the moment.

'Can you say how many people have died yet?'

'Right now there are four people who are confirmed dead and they're estimating the injured to be about three hundred.'

'And how many people have been evacuated from the two buildings?'

'They're still doing it. All the power is down and people are coming from the 100-and-something floor. They have to walk.'

'How many people are in these buildings?' I asked.

'They don't know. There's no way to know. It's in the thou-sands, in the tens of thousands of people who are in these buildings. As you can see, the damage is all around us; it's not just isolated.'

I thought it was odd that Ed kept saying 'they don't know' and 'they're still doing it', as though the rescue operation were someone else's responsibility. I thought perhaps he was ashamed of what had happened. I couldn't understand why he made it sound as if he weren't involved and he didn't define who 'they' were, and why they remained anonymous. Neither of us could begin to comprehend the full significance of that day, and what would follow in the coming years. This was a major disaster and he should be part of the operation and its investigation, but he seemed to know very little. All the marshals I came into contact with that day didn't appear to be taking any direct role in the investigation.

Mike came over and stood to my left. His helmet was on, but his fire tunic was open, the collar of his formal white shirt pushing up through the top of his patterned crew neck sweater. The chatter was repeatedly interrupted by the clanging sound of falling metal echoing across the bomb site.

'There may be more bodies, more people in the rubble. We've established these cars are empty,' said Mike, turning to point at the wreckage behind him. 'And this happened at lunchtime. In the floors beneath us there are offices, rooms, with people in them, eating sandwiches. It's just amazing there are not more dead.'

With my experience, I could not imagine that well over 1,000 feet above us people were still waiting to be rescued about seven hours after the bomb exploded. I pressed Mike on the firefighting operation.

'How long before you finish evacuating the building?'

'I have no idea,' he replied. 'There are no elevators. Some people can't take the stress of walking. You can't operate a building of a 100 stories with no elevator.'

'Are they still using helicopters to evacuate people from the roof?' I asked,

'When I came in there was a chopper on the roof, but I don't know if it's in use.' He looked across to two Port Authority Police Officers, 'They don't brief me,' he said. 'Why don't you ask them?' He also seemed quite vague about the incident, but this was exactly the sort of job he would usually investigate. Some of the wrecked cars had just been damaged or moved by the force, but there had been a serious fire. I was intrigued.

Ed then pointed out another column with a long chunk of yellow-painted kerbstone sticking out from above us and sloping downwards at an angle. A crew of firefighters carrying heavy axes passed us and stopped to examine the column. On the other side of the void I saw the flashing indicator light of one of the ghost cars, bright orange pulsing in time with feedback squealing from the firefighters' radios.

'The devastation is all around us, Clifford. Look: it's all the way around,' said Ed.

'Next stop, we'll go down to a lower level and you can see the extent of the explosion,' said Mike.

'What? You mean the lower levels are worse?' asked one of the cops.

'No, it's not worse, but the walls are bent in. It's just a surprise how far the shock wave has travelled.'

We walked to the corridor, and down another flight of stairs. We were now in basement level three. We could only walk a little way into the car park as this floor was blocked by hundreds of feet of pipework that had collapsed onto the floor and buckled, shearing it away from the columns that were meant to support it. I shone the camera light through a gap in the tangle of metal spaghetti. The light caught a yellow reflective sign showing a stick man and warning drivers of pedestrians, an eerie image. There were no firefighters or cops working in the third basement level, just Hester, Jon, Mike and I. There was the occasional piercing sound coming from a car alarm. Some of the car park columns were buckling under the strain, and several cars were buried by the pipework. Suddenly, from close behind us, there was an enormous crash of falling metal, although we couldn't see where it came from.

'That's enough for me!' said Mike, who pointed out the bowing walls as we left. 'The devastation here is hard to believe,' he continued, concerned but calm.

I could see piles of large concrete building blocks, broken

and scattered over the floor. I looked up at the wall, which was coated in an even layer of black soot from the explosion and fire. It reminded me of the scores of fires that I had been to where a small fire in one room could cause smoke damage to the whole house.

The wall was etched with cracks, suggesting a risk of further collapse. We walked around the building, and Mike pointed out the ramp that led from the third level to the second. We were now on the opposite side of the crater, directly underneath where we first entered. Mike stopped and picked up a warped piece of sheet metal, about 8ft by 6ft long.

'This is the hood of a white Thunderbird, although we can't find one,' he said.

'Really? Where did it come from?' I asked as Mike dropped the metal, the noise masking my question.

'What's that?'

'Has it come down?' I asked.

'You tell me. It's come from the middle of that pile – that's how far it's been thrown. Where the original car is it's too early to tell. It obviously has to be in the middle of that pile of mess. That's the force of the explosion. The shock waves are indicated by these walls,' he said, looking to his left.

We worked our way up towards the exit at street level, retracing our steps. When we reached the first basement level, Mike stopped to show us more damaged walls. We were several hundred feet from the explosion's epicentre, but its force had blown open doors in a locker room.

'It's amazing there aren't more casualties – more fatalities,' said Mike.

Jon had picked up some news of the evacuation. 'They estimate about 8,000 people in each tower,' he said as we approached the stairs up to the exit.

Hester filmed our last moments. As we reached the doors, Jon told us to stop filming. 'You don't want to piss off the American media, do you? Because they're not allowed in here.'

'Right,' replied Hester, who seemed a bit put out by the request.

'I don't want to piss anyone off,' I said, so we agreed to stop filming at least until we were outside the Vista Hotel. We still had the rest of the night ahead of us with the Bronx marshals. We looked up at the World Trade Center's North Tower, which had an inconsistent scattering of lights on some of the tower's 110 floors. There were fire trucks parked in front of the entrance and the drone of engines and generators. The front lobby of the Vista was lit by a large portable floodlight unit.

The Brooklyn marshal was waiting for us. We walked a short way before he stopped to talk to an exhausted-looking fire crew. Some had their tunics off and they had blackened faces. I was unable to hear the conversation, but then the marshal turned to me and said, 'They walked up to the 75th floor. They're still doing a search.'

'Is it a primary search?' he asked one of the firefighters. I thought this was impossible; they must have searched the tower by now. *Why was there so much confusion and uncertainty?* I didn't dare ask the question as these firefighters didn't look too enthusiastic about me being there.

'No, a secondary – we just completed a secondary search,' said the firefighter to the Brooklyn marshal and I saw an opportunity.

'What's it like up there?' I shouted above the engine noise, my question either unheard or ignored by the six men crewing a giant hydraulic platform.

'What's it like up there?'

'Hot. Dirty,' came the abrupt reply from one of the fire-fighters. They turned away and climbed onto their truck, clearly not keen to speak. They looked upset. It was getting late. The ice was packed hard on the sidewalk as we walked towards the Brooklyn marshal's car. We headed north, away from the bombing and towards the Bronx to meet up with the marshals at the base there for our planned filming.

I could not stop thinking about Ed's words: 'This is New York City – we're not at war with anybody.' I realised that I was now an outsider, no longer a rescue worker, but I'd been to the centre of another major disaster, the effects of which were rippling around the world on television and radio news programmes. Did the exhausted hydraulic platform crew think I was an irritating member of the press? They obviously didn't know that I used to do the same job they did, but my status – as a constituent part of the triangle holding it all together – had gone.

I also realised that it would be impossible to forget my fire-service training. I had been thinking through all the rescue scenarios the entire day but my role had changed. There was a certain pointlessness about the whole thing: we had great pictures, but we couldn't use them. The next day was a Saturday; there'd only be a handful of short news bulletins in the UK over the weekend. What if I scooped everybody and sold them for a fortune, then missed out on the chance to make my documentary? And was Stickevers bluffing? Would they seriously not let me back into the United States ever again?

It was hard to understand how someone could plan such a massive disaster, but later details emerged. At 12:18, in the middle of lunchtime that day, two Islamist terrorists drove a yellow Ryder van into the underground car park on West

Street, through a large rectangular entrance close to the Vista Hotel. The tower had six basements, and the car park was deep below the surface; it was possible to park as far down as the fourth level. The fifth level contained a large refrigeration room, the sixth housed tunnels for the Port Authority Trans Hudson railway line and emergency generators for the towers.

The terrorists filled the van with a cocktail of explosives including a urea-nitrate (fertiliser) bomb, weighing more than 1,300 pounds, made all the more lethal by using hydrogen gas cylinders to enhance the effect. The bombers drove the van into the second basement level of the North Tower, their intention to position it at the outer edge so that when detonated it would cause the building to topple into the South Tower, causing both to collapse.

When the bomb went off, it blew a large hole through the floor of the second basement level, sending debris down to the third basement and then through existing open spaces into the fourth level, culminating in a massive pile of rubble landing at the fifth basement level. The shock wave caused damage to the emergency generators and a large pipe from the adjacent Hudson River burst, flooding the area.

The explosion also blew a hole about 60ft by 80ft upward through the ceiling of level two into the floor of basement level one. The force blew another hole through the concourse of the 22-storey Vista Hotel, and shattered a glass partition wall, allowing the smoke to fill the North Tower. With no power, there were no elevators so thousands of people were trapped. The attack killed six people and injured over a 1000, but it also caused political and psychological tremors that sent a chilling message across the world. The events of that day heralded a new dawn of terror and fear.

CHAPTER 9

An Arrest in Queens

I intended to visit New York to find out about the marshals. I was intrigued about the armed firefighters who investigated arson and tracked down its perpetrators, but I found myself caught up in a massive news story. On the night of the bomb, Hester and I returned to the Bronx Base escorted by two of the marshals. We had over a week left in which to gather enough pictures to convince a production company in the UK that the unique firefighters' story was worth telling in a documentary. I felt as if I'd been handed this massive scoop, but didn't have enough journalistic or documentary experience to know what to do with what I had. I hoped my rushes would be taken seriously, but I also had to learn the craft of a new industry – an immense challenge.

With so many suspicious fires every day in the city, we knew there was a chance that we'd come across either a stiff or an arrest. Over the course of the week we worked various shifts assigned to a different squad so we got to know the 30 marshals at the Bronx base. We filmed their every step day and night.

A few days after the bombing, we were filming one night with two marshals. Driving through the Bronx with its run-down tenement blocks and bustling shops we saw a red flare fizzing in the middle of a main road. Standing in front of it was a cop and, seeing a crime scene, the marshals drove up to him as one of them flashed his shield.

'What you got, buddy?'

'Hi. Not a lot – just one down.'

'Bad guy I hope?'

'Yep, he's a bad guy – dead too.'

The exchange took seconds and the Lincoln drove off, diverted around the body which I could see out of the window covered in a coat. It wasn't so much the fact that someone was dead that shocked me, but the complete lack of emotion, excitement or concern in the exchange between the marshals and the cop.

I wanted to really make a name for myself as a journalist and documentary maker, and cruising the five boroughs reinforced the feeling of being inside an especially unique group of firefighters. The banter and camaraderie was the same as when I was a fireman in London.

That night we were dispatched to a fire call, which required a squad (two marshals in a car) to investigate. We drove through a street in midtown Manhattan and I could see prostitutes walking up and down the sidewalk, oblivious to the unmarked car. As the marshal gave a blast from the siren, the women, realising the car contained law enforcement officers, scurried off into blackened doorways even though we were not even going to stop. Inside the car, the chatter of the fire department radio was competing with country-and-western music from a tape player on the dashboard. It was a surreal scene, and with the horrors of my past behind me, I was enjoying the anonymity, the excitement and my first experience of being undercover.

I was growing more and more intrigued by the marshals' peculiar job of putting on their fire gear to turn over the smouldering embers looking for signs of arson, then following their leads in civilian detective clothes.

What makes someone turn to arson? I thought. In seven years as a firefighter I'd never knowingly come face-to-face with a fire-starter. What would drive someone to inflict damage that has such destructive qualities? Someone with a grudge could take out their anger on a victim's car by damaging it. They could attack their target with the intention of giving them a scare, or physically harm them. But fire takes on a life of its own. It has no respect for the hand that ignites it, and no limit to its spread, devouring property, possessions and lives.

About five days into the trip we were out with Fire Marshals Lynch and Monzillo. Lynch was a tall, quiet, wiry man with greying hair and terrible fashion sense, but his calmness masked the mind of a detective constantly analysing every potential clue. Monzillo was Mediterranean-looking with a thin black moustache and bald head, and someone who looked like he did things by the book.

We were called to investigate a fire in a truck parked outside a warehouse in the Bronx. It was a bright day, but the wind whipped off Long Island Sound. Monzillo and Lynch were gathering burnt fragments and putting them into an evidence can – about the size of a biscuit tin. A young black man was talking to them, jabbering away.

Among the debris he found a scorched Bible, and that made him speak even faster, horrified by the thought of someone burning such sacred words. The marshals requested the fire department's photographer, who, with the most basic camera, took some pictures of the scene. The investigation seemed futile. They had no equipment for detecting petrol or other fuel used as an accelerant, which I had seen used in London on many occasions. Their job looked pointless. *How could this lead to an arrest?* I wondered.

Then another squad called Monzillo on the radio. They were investigating a small fire at a hostel in Queens and had called in a code 10-41, signalling that the fire was suspicious. They were about to make an arrest, so Monzillo and Lynch abandoned the warehouse job and we headed for the neighbouring borough.

We were going to the Crystal Hotel, at 88 Beach 102nd Street, in the Far Rockaway neighbourhood, close to John F. Kennedy Airport. Monzillo and Lynch, like all the city's fire marshals, started their careers as firefighters, seeing themselves as firefighters with police powers. But it was this odd juxtaposition of careers that made them so fascinating. I couldn't get my head around the idea of a firefighter being issued with a gun.

The Crystal Hotel lacked a concierge, flash lobby and uniformed staff. It was managed by Bobby – a scruffy man in his mid-50s with a brash voice and a groaning gut hanging over filthy brown trousers. It was more hostel then hotel, in a rundown, windswept strip of land to the west of Long Island.

I sat in the back of the Lincoln with Hester, eager to see the marshals make an arrest. As we arrived at the hotel, there was no sign of fire, just scorched mattresses outside the building, but their job was to establish if a fire had been started deliberately, then find the perpetrator.

We entered the lobby, where there was an Hispanic woman in her late 20s sitting on a bench. She looked pale and had dark rings around her eyes, a bandana on her head, and was wearing a black top zipped-up to her neck, and jeans. Lynch stood sentry over her in his detective clothes: leather bomber jacket, white shirt and tie, Smith & Wesson revolver concealed in its holster, his shield hung from a chain around his neck. Monzillo went straight to the hotel's office, talking to Bobby out of sight.

The woman was incoherent and babbling about a mattress and pillows. Someone she knew had started a fire, she was telling Lynch. He looked straight ahead, non-committal in his silence.

Then Monzillo emerged from the office with a stern look on his face. He had a notebook in his hand with a typed script on the cover. As he stood over the woman, it was clear that he thought she was responsible for a crime.

'Listen, before you make any more statements we have to read you your rights. Do you understand that? You don't have to make any more statements – do you understand that?' said Monzillo, while Lynch maintained his pose.

'What do you mean, you're arresting me?' the woman asked anxiously.

'We are arresting you.'

'But I didn't do anything.' It was clear the woman, now the focus of the 'crime', was disturbed; Monzillo's tone was authoritarian but calm.

'OK fine, we have to work this out. This is my job: I have to do what I have to do. Just relax.' He crouched alongside the woman, eyes level with hers.

Her voice cracked. She interrupted, 'But I have to call my parents...'

'Fine, no problem, alright, you can make the phone calls later. Just listen to your rights as I read them to you: you have the right to remain silent and not to answer any questions, you don't have to talk to me – do you understand that? Understand?'

'Yes, sir.'

'OK, anything you say may be used against you in a court of law – do you understand that?'

'Yes.'

I watched the imminent arrest, standing behind Hester, who was filming the scene. I felt helpless, as I knew this woman was about to lose her liberty, but I didn't have any qualms about filming the exchange, somewhat enjoying my new role and convinced it was in the public interest.

'You have the right to consult with an attorney before speaking to the fire marshal – and to have an attorney present during any questioning. Do you understand?' Monzillo continued and the woman nodded. 'If you can't afford it, one will be provided without cost – do you understand that?'

It was clear she was struggling to make sense of the long list of rights, but continued to answer 'yes', or nod and fidget.

'OK, if you do not have an attorney available, you have the right to remain silent until you've had the opportunity to consult with one. Do you understand?'

The woman stood up and walked towards the office. Monzillo grabbed her right arm.

'I'm just going...' Her words faded and she began to sob. Bobby took hold of her in the office, where she began crying uncontrollably.

'They want to make sure you see a doctor,' said Bobby.

Monzillo entered the office. 'We have to do this for you.'

'OK, you're gonna go with them.' Bobby's voice was loud but calm, giving the impression that he dealt with such matters regularly and was familiar with the procedure. I got the impression that Bobby knew that her arrest would also be the only way of the woman getting the help she needed and prevent more serious issues at his hostel.

'I don't want to go with them,' she pleaded.

'I know you don't.'

At that point Monzillo turned around to face me. He shook

his head, and raised his left hand indicating that we'd seen enough and it was time to stop filming. Then he shut the door.

About 10 minutes later Bobby and the marshals – Lynch with a lit cigarette in his hand – walked out of the Crystal Hotel, with the woman handcuffed behind her back forcing her to stoop and struggle with the hotel's steps. She was helped into the scratched Lincoln by Lynch and taken to the local police precinct, then escorted to Central Booking in Manhattan, where she was arraigned and charged with arson.

By the end of my trip, I'd built up a good knowledge of the FDNY. The marshals with their powers of arrest were unique and the idea of carrying guns was controversial. Much of the Bronx was a no-go area for white people at the time, but the firefighters, who were mostly white, protected the borough the same as they would the other four. Both London firefighters and their New York counterparts had a very strong pedigree. London had built up extensive firefighting experience during the Blitz. Likewise, New York had the experience of the burning tenement blocks in the 1970s, where some firehouses could lose one or more firefighters on a night shift to injury. I respected the approaches of both cities to the art of firefighting, but the unifying factor was the spirit and determination of the crews.

The trip had been fascinating, but when I returned to London with a taste for a new career, my own firefighting days felt like they were drifting deep into the past. My training notes, diaries, and the uniform I was allowed to keep were boxed up and put into storage.

I lost contact with all the firefighters I served with, and never went back on a London fire station. Although I'd built up considerable experience, passed promotion exams, and returned to college, it all felt wasted. As my journalistic experience grew, I found it harder to talk about what I'd experienced – it all seemed so irrelevant now, and I didn't want to relive anything that had happened during my seven years firefighting, eager to leave my past behind while managing my symptoms.

The original producer who'd helped me with the marshals project, and had let me do some research in his office, had lost interest. So I showed my rushes from the filming trip to several producers and directors, but didn't have the experience or confidence to develop my ideas. I locked the tapes away, frustrated by being presented with a unique opportunity that had come so soon in my new career. But throughout 1993, I continued in my efforts to get into the television industry, and by the summer, was working on a music programme for a satellite broadcaster in the UK, which distanced me from documentary film-making. It was at times frustrating, but I also felt great satisfaction from working with pictures; filming and working on recorded items and although I still suffered many symptoms of the PTSD, things were more stable – but my symptoms worsened again in the summer of 1993 and I didn't work for several months. Even when I did it was on a freelance basis or short-term contract.

I needed to be pushed, and best of all was the live TV studio environment, which had some of the same buzz and adrenaline as the fire ground.

I felt as though my career to date was divided into two halves and I had little certainty ahead of me. I'd set my heart on my new career, but it would take until 1997 – another four years – before I got even close to my new dream and the security it would bring. In the meantime I'd begun to wonder what had happened to Gordon's family. But the heat and smoke were long in the past, that skill and experience would never be relevant or useful again.

At least that's what I thought.

PART THREE: Making the News
London, 1999 to 2010

We can see and understand only a little about God now,
as if we were peering at his reflection in a poor mirror,
but someday we are going to see him in his completeness,
face to face.
Now all that I know is hazy and blurred,
but then I will see everything clearly,
just as clearly as God sees into my heart right now.

I Corinthians 13:12

CHAPTER 10

Paddington

Journalists depend on their sources, but abide by a universal code of never revealing their sources.

I can't explain the decision I made on the morning of 5 October 1999, when I drove out of the car park at BBC Television Centre, in west London, eyes stinging and exhausted after another night shift. I felt like I had a hangover without the enjoyment of a few drinks and a good laugh the night before.

It was 10 past eight in the morning. The rest of my team, including Sean, my shift-mate and canteen confidant, and prickly Alexia-Jane, the night editor, were still working on the morning's news. The barrier went up; I looked left, I looked right. I hesitated and then turned right. Within 20 minutes I was on the Embankment, by the River Thames, heading for home and sleep. Turning right was always the safer option. It avoided the elevated section of the A40 heading into town and my fear of falling asleep in a massive concrete chute in bumper-to-bumper traffic.

Then the call came. A trusted source, words that struck me with excitement and trepidation. Words that cancelled the 'hangover', fired my pulse and flooded my body with adrenaline: 'There's a suspected bomb near Paddington – some kind of explosion... stand by. Reports of smoke going up... OK. It's confirmed. The Metropolitan Police have initiated major incident procedure: train crash, Ladbroke Grove, W10, multiple casualties.'

My source was 100% reliable.

Six years had passed since the trip to New York and filming with the marshals. I clung on to the idea that my rushes of the World Trade Center bombing could eventually be worked into a more professionally produced documentary, but the bombing and my experience with the arson detectives had been the only time until now that my two careers crossed over. In the meantime, I needed to earn money.

I worked on a number of low-budget student films, and as a volunteer runner, on the BBC's *Hearts of Gold* series with Esther Rantzen, to get experience. It was a completely different environment to that of a firefighter. I was so used to being told what to do, obeying orders, wearing a standard uniform. But when I worked on films, I was surrounded by people coming up with ideas in a creative environment. I'd never worked with women before, except a couple of shifts when a female firefighter was sent to provide cover at Stratford. But now I was surrounded by women: running make-up departments and the production design. Many were directors and producers. I no longer played up to the hero; no one was interested in that.

I was at the lowest end of the career scale in my 'new' industry, and often one of only a few men in a team of women. I worked in a world where everyone was well educated, and I was still only part way through my degree, eventually graduating in 1994. Despite my work with the marshals in New York, I felt that my experience as a firefighter didn't count for anything. In later years this would become so extreme that I worked out entire contracts on programmes for many months without ever revealing my previous job as a firefighter. I felt it was irrelevant and I was starting every day from scratch. But I gradually began to realise that there were similarities to working on a television programme and on a fire, in terms of planning and working under pressure.

By 1993, I was 26 and had begun working with a freelance cameraman, and we started to shoot our own stories. Both the BBC and ITV were happy in those days to pay freelancers to gather elements of a story while their reporter stayed at base. It was invaluable experience that helped me pave my way into broadcast journalism.

I'd fallen in love with New York and would visit once or twice a year. I loved the sense of escapism; everyone there was trying to be an actor, writer or director, which allowed me to be part of a new world. I relished the distance from my old life. I briefly explored the possibility of applying for a green card, although I knew it would be hard to work there. I still hadn't formed a new relationship but I'd met plenty of friends in the City, where socialising came much easier.

In 1994 I landed a contract job at the BBC on its former television arts programme *The Late Show*. It was a fairly basic role, involving answering the phones and booking post-production facilities, but it was permanent work albeit on a contract. By the following summer, the programme was axed and my contract wasn't renewed. I was coping much better with my symptoms, but I was still years behind some of the young and very talented presenters and producers I worked alongside. It was at times like these that I still felt very much the former firefighter: the 'man who was'. I could have given up, but by now I'd set my heart on a career in television.

I decided I wanted to focus on news programmes, and after a few years of freelancing, short-term contracts and a job as a researcher for BBC's *Newsnight* programme, I worked for BBC News 24 (now the BBC News Channel), moving on to *Breakfast TV* in 2000. I picked up the craft of journalism as I went along, and the BBC provided training, eventually moving up the ladder to broadcast journalist, looking after many of the creative and technical elements of what went on 'behind the scenes': from writing presenter briefs to editing headlines, booking guests and sourcing locations. I'd always imagined myself being in front of the camera as a presenter or reporter. It was perhaps a fantasy linked to my old job, where we had some notoriety. But as I settled into my new career, the appeal of being on-screen faded. The lack of confidence I felt, and continue to feel, is a tiny fraction of my former brave, courageous self. I feel it has truly held me back as I live with the legacy of my fear: *What if something goes wrong?*

Had I turned left I'd have been practically alongside the 08:06 from Paddington to Bedwyn in Wiltshire, as it collided head-on with a First Great Western high-speed train which exploded. The combined speed on impact was 132 miles per hour.

I parked in Ladbroke Grove and phoned the news desk.

'Hello, BBC News 24.'

'It's Cliff. I'm at Ladbroke Grove. It's a train crash and they've declared a major incident.'

'We've got the weather camera trained live on some smoke – err, an explosion? A bomb?' It was Sean.

'No, it's a train crash – I'm there. Definitely a train crash.'

'Cliff, stay on the line. Where are you exactly?'

'The Silver Command position, in Barlby Road.'

I was standing in the middle of yet another catastrophe, another urban war zone: roaring generators, bristling uniforms, a rising column of grey smoke, and trails of blood everywhere. There were bodies on stretchers against shopfronts, and it was impossible to tell victim from onlooker: the worried, the weary and the bloody in an enormous amalgam of desperate humanity.

'OK, Cliff. Don't hang up, mate. We're putting you on-air.'

I was shaking, and cold, but absorbed as much colour of the scene as I could, mobile phone pressed to my ear as I struggled to block out the noise of disaster.

'Clifford – hi, it's studio N8 sound desk. Can you hear me?'

'Yes, got you.'

'OK, you should be getting programme audio now...'

'I can't hear it. It's too quiet!'

A squadron of paramedics in green overalls hauling massive medical kits in rucksacks marched by.

'OK... Better?' asked the sound engineer.

'Yes, I can hear. Who's the presenter, and what am I following?'

'N8 to Clifford – it's Alexia-Jane, can you hear me? Thirty seconds to you. It's Ben Geoghegan two-waying you.'

I'd had just about enough time to take in the scene, deafened as every type of emergency vehicle imaginable descended on Barlby Road. I kept thinking of what my mate Al, who has never been an emergency-service worker or a journalist, always used to say, 'When you get a second wind, make the most of it, because you won't get a third.' I hung on to that second wind with every shivering fibre of my body.

'Now I think we can talk to our reporter, Clifford Thompson, who's at Barlby Road police control centre.' Ben was calm and reassuring.

'Yes, good morning, Ben. I can tell you that the police are getting set up here for a very long operation. There are about

20 or 30 ambulances here at the fire, police and medical control point… I've just seen one young man walk up to a police officer and say "I've just come off that train". It's getting more organised but there are still people coming out from where the crash is.'

'What can you see?'

'There are probably about 150 fire and police officers here… The ambulance service have just confirmed to me that they are now working to their major incident plan.'

'Are people still coming off the trains?'

'Yes, there are still people wandering around the scene. As I got here, the police closed Ladbroke Grove right the way up its entire length… There's one middle-aged man, face covered in soot, waiting by a fire engine – he's sustained head injuries and the police are arranging an escort to get him away.'

'What can you see of the crash site?'

'There's a pall of smoke rising into the air.'

We finished the interview and immediately my phone rang. It was a colleague from one of the radio networks, so I ran through all the facts again, live on-air. The radio producer told me they were running a phone-in programme but that I should call if there were any developments.

The police said they would allow a group of journalists to go down to the tracks, escorted by them. This was an unusual step as such disasters are treated as crime scenes with efforts to preserve the tiniest bits of evidence. They opened a gate and led us through as I pushed my way to the front. There was blood spattered all over the weeds, the dirt and the tracks. One carriage, which had been at the heart of the fire, had erupted following the crash and was now ashen grey and stripped of paint. It looked like the car I'd seen in the bombed basement of the World Trade Center. Later it emerged this was the notorious 'Coach H', which contained the bodies of many victims, reduced to ash in the fragile structure of the buckled carriage.

We were about 50ft from the wreck and the silence was broken as scores of mobile phones were placed to ears with cries of, 'News desk: I've got colour for you from the train crash,' and 'I'm standing by the burned-out carriage...' and 'I need to file from the train disaster. I've got copy to file.' I calmly lifted my phone and called into the radio network as Nicky Campbell broke away from one of the callers to his BBC *Radio Five Live* phone-in show to talk to me on-air.

A few minutes later I met a cameraman who'd been shooting the first pictures on tape from very close to the crash scene. He handed me the cassette and I ran for about half a mile to the satellite truck parked up in a side street outside the cordon. The first pictures from the edge of the crash were played out live as around us emergency-service workers ran in every direction.

I returned to the crash site several times over the coming days as we followed every step of the rescue, the recovery and the clear-up.

The crash killed 31 people and injured 520. It was remarkably similar to the 1988 Clapham train crash in scale, which killed 35 and injured 500. It was six years since the World Trade Center bombing, but my experience as a firefighter had really helped – especially in the first day or so with my expert eye on the emergency services' body language and knowledge of their procedures. Even though I'd worked all night at the BBC, I felt superhuman, full of adrenaline as I ran with the tapes to get those first close-up pictures on-air.

On the afternoon of the first day of the incident, my boss called at home to congratulate me on my work. Another colleague heard one of my interviews and said I sounded nervous, but that had added to the drama.

I was at the heart of another major disaster. When things calmed down, I analysed how I felt before I went to work the night shift, and how I'd made sure I was organised and prepared. It's easy to be wise after the event, but I'm convinced there was something: a warning, a change in mood, a feeling of foreboding. Around many of the disasters I've experienced, I've felt the need to tidy things up – check in with useful contacts and plan my time, as if something is about to happen. As a firefighter, I hated going to work and leaving unfinished business, or parting company with friends and family on bad terms – just in case anything should happen to me.

It felt strange to have witnessed so many tragedies, but I was confident that by 1999, when the Paddington train crash happened, my career change had been worthwhile. I had become an expert on fires, train crashes and bombs. At Paddington, I reported live on events in contrast to my earlier years, when I was so involved in the rescue operation that it was almost impossible to comprehend the wider context.

By this stage in my life I had settled down, emotionally. I was no longer having therapy and was becoming more integrated in my new career, which had helped me move from my studio flat into a four-bedroom townhouse in the Docklands with a girlfriend, with whom I was trying to make a go of things.

Word got around about my past as a firefighter and I'd be asked by other journalists for my opinion on a disaster, or some policy issue on the fire service. While I was a lot more open and able to talk about my experiences, I still wasn't ready to go back and look at the past, find the characters I'd worked with, or the victims. My diaries, notes, and copies of reports remained in a box. Every day, I thought about the fire in which Gordon died, and I imagined him watching over me from above.

I began to wonder if false memory had taken over and skewed my recollection of that fire, just before Christmas 1991. On one hand Eton Road was so vivid, but had the distance of time made me remember it less clearly? Maybe I had over-exaggerated events, or made them out to be more serious than they were. Perhaps I never played as important a role as I thought I had. Bringing it all back to the surface, especially with regard to tracing Gordon's family, was difficult. Memories would become real people, and all the buried emotions might resurface. It was going to be the hardest assignment yet.

What could be harder than investigating myself?

CHAPTER 11

King's Cross - 2007

Elmer's car was a large Mercedes estate, a classic design probably from the late 1980s. It was around nine in the morning, and he'd returned to the car with a cup of tea for me in a polystyrene cup, but he had forgotten to get me a lid. I was sitting in the passenger seat, anxious to get going. We had a long day ahead of us and Elmer and I were going to make a short film, including several interviews.

We were parked outside the newsroom on the ring road that lassoed BBC Television Centre in White City. There was nowhere for me to rest the cup so I blew into the tea impatiently in an attempt to cool it down.

'Thanks for the tea.'

'That's OK – sorry about the lid.'

'No worries, but we need to get going soon. Our first location is Buckingham – just outside, in fact.'

'For 10:30? We'll be OK,' said Elmer.

I never really looked too closely at the fires I attended that were reported by the media. There was sometimes a brief report in the local newspaper; bigger incidents occasionally made the national news. It had been 15 years since I fought my last fire and technology had moved on considerably. In the early 1990s, mobile phones fitted into vehicles were still a new concept, as was the fax machine. The fire-station teleprinter made way for the faster computer printer for receiving emergency calls. As I grappled my way into a new career as a journalist, information became more freely available with the growth of the Internet and the rise of cheaper computers. I had access to powerful databases and elaborate archives.

When I was a firefighter it was often impossible to get any real context about an incident beyond what I could see or hear, but there was so much more information available by the turn of the millennium.

It was early November 2007, and the 20th anniversary of the King's Cross fire was on the horizon. I decided to look back 20 years and find out more about the fire, its victims and the investigation. I told my editor that I was keen to produce a report to mark the anniversary. She said I had to find a story; we couldn't cover it just because it was 20 years ago.

About a year after the Paddington train crash, I moved over to BBC Breakfast Television, where I worked as a TV journalist. It was a permanent job and, now in my 40s, I felt established. I was single again – I'd bought a flat after splitting with my ex-girlfriend – and had little prospect of settling down. But I liked being independent again, living on my own and being self-contained. Having to only think and worry about myself suited me, and insulated me. I would travel by myself and took to hiding away, whenever I could, on a Caribbean island. But I was living the island life whether at home or abroad, struggling to let anyone join me. I wanted to be solely responsible for myself, and be protected from my past.

Although I lost contact with most of my old colleagues I did keep in touch with one or two, after going to the retirement function for a station officer I had worked with who left the brigade in 2005. That was just after a turbulent time of national strikes by firefighters in 2002 and 2003, following a highly-critical review of the fire service in the UK by Professor George Bain.

An unprecedented test of the London Fire Brigade's skill came later in the summer of 2005. The multiple terrorist attacks in July led to a series of government reports; the victims' inquests came much later. As I searched my way through some recent stories I kept seeing references in the 7 July attacks to King's Cross and the failure to implement the recommendations made in 1988. If some of these had been implemented, it was suggested, it might have helped in the devastation of the summer of 2005. I discovered that the full public inquiry report for the King's Cross fire, by Sir Desmond Fennell QC, had been posted on a railway information website. I printed it off and spent several evenings working late reading the two-inch-thick report, comparing what Sir Desmond had recommended with what had been implemented – or what was still outstanding.

One issue kept recurring: the inability of firefighters working on the surface to communicate with their colleagues underground, or to the other emergency services whether on the surface or underground.

My first task was to track down Sir Desmond. I found his name listed in a central London chamber of barristers. I called the clerk, who said he would pass my details on to him but that he had retired. Then one evening, just as I was about to leave the office, he called and agreed to let me interview him at his home near Buckingham.

Elmer and I sat on the M1 in heavy traffic. I called Sir Desmond and told him we'd be late, terrified that I might miss my chance. I had read up on the fire, set aside my own experience of the night and was keen to find out why there were still so many issues that hadn't been addressed 20 years later. We had had two other interviews later the same day, with a former Metropolitan Police inspector who had been on duty during the night of the fire, and a woman whose brother was killed there.

The wintry sun hung low over the motorway as we peeled off and followed a series of winding lanes and minor roads. It wasn't until the Mercedes's wheels crunched over the gravel drive that I knew my filming would be safe. We were greeted at the door by Sir Desmond's assistant, who showed us into the beautiful detached Georgian mansion. We sat in the lounge and she brought us milky coffee and some fancy chocolate biscuits.

I had spent weeks preparing for this. I knew the story inside out and felt confident that a retired high court judge, praised for his inquiry into the fire and now shocked by the failure to implement his recommendations, would make a great story. I felt the responsibility of speaking on behalf of the 31 people who died, the scores who were injured and the dozens of emergency workers, their careers cut short by the enormous trauma. It had taken a lot to persuade the sister of a man killed in the fire to be interviewed again, but she said she was swayed by my unique position of having been a firefighter and so she was now telling her family's story. Sir Desmond felt the same.

We chatted as Elmer positioned the lights. Sir Desmond told me he had retired after having a stroke some years before.

'OK, I'm ready, Clifford,' said Elmer. He crouched and positioned his eye to the viewfinder, pressed the record button and on came the red light.

'Sir Desmond, you went down into the fire shortly after. What was it like?'

He hesitated. 'My impression was absolute horror. The devastation, with the smell of acrylic and burnt wood was absolutely appalling. It was like going down a black hole into a bloody hell. The thought of the injury and panic that must have gone through the people on the escalator was absolutely horrific – almost too much to contemplate.'

The hair stood up on the back of my neck as he told the story. He was as calm and composed as one would expect a High Court judge to be, but for a few seconds he was unsettled, reliving the horror – passionate about the terrible circumstances in which so many died.

'Your public inquiry made lots of recommendations, including the issue of communication. What did you think about that?'

'The essence of it was a lack of control and command. There was no communication at all. Those who were on the surface couldn't tell what was happening beneath them. That was the heart of it.'

He was referring to London Underground's procedures at the time, which meant when there was an incident, details were passed from a member of staff to a supervisor, without any practical help being given. At the fire, there was a long delay before a fire extinguisher was used on what started as a small, smouldering fire, and the technology did not exist to allow radios to work underground.

'Twenty years later, how do you feel about the fact that there are still problems communicating on the Underground?' I asked.

'I feel despondent about it. I daresay that there are technical problems, but if the Americans can communicate with a man on the moon then it seems extraordinary that the Brits can't establish a system that will get people talking 20 yards beneath the surface.'

The government appointed Desmond Fennell to lead the public inquiry less than a week after the King's Cross tragedy. There was some surprise at his selection. He was an active member of the Conservative Party and some thought he was too close to Prime Minister Margaret Thatcher's government. He had been chair of the party in Buckingham, and in the 1960s had led a campaign opposed to building a new airport that was being proposed to serve London, but located in Buckinghamshire. When the plans were abandoned in 1971, it was reported in the press that he led a torch-lit celebration through the village of Stewkley.

When he was appointed to lead the inquiry, Fennell was 54, a barrister and recorder, or junior judge. It was commented on in the press that the inquiry might be chaired by 'someone more senior'.

A former Grenadier Guardsman, Fennell had one particularly notable case on his CV: he'd been part of the prosecution team that saw the conviction in 1964 of the Great Train Robbers. On his appointment to chair the inquiry he said he was 'enormously flattered ... to chair the public inquiry into such a horrific disaster' and that it would be 'satisfying and challenging to establish what had happened and make sure it never happened again'.

I tried to imagine how he would have looked as a silk in his wig and robes. His calm and quiet voice must have put fear into those he was prosecuting and sending to prison, but he was the perfect gentleman. He wore a smart country style, cream check shirt, and a black cardigan.

I continued with my questions. 'Did you hope your recommendations would lead to change?'

'That's the one I wanted most of all: I wanted to change the relationship between the fire brigade and London Underground. The Underground did not understand what the task of the fire brigade was, and the fire brigade had not been prepared or done any reconnaissance. One wanted to establish a better spirit between the two and a better cooperation. I think that will have now come about, but I don't know.'

'Who should have been responsible to make sure these changes happened?' I asked.

'London Underground were responsible for the communications, but the fire brigade ought to have known how to approach the place, how to get in and out, and they might, with greater speed, to have been able to save more people.'

'If you look at the 150 or more recommendations, who should have been responsible for making sure all of them were implemented?'

'There was a specific recommendation that London Underground should implement the recommendations and should report to the secretary of state from time to time to demonstrate how they were getting on.'

On 10 November 1988, less than a year after the fire, Desmond Fennell's 247-page report was ready to be presented to Parliament. Expecting it to be highly critical of London Underground, the chairman of London Regional Transport, Sir Keith Bright, resigned and later that morning its chief executive, Dr Tony Ridley, followed suit. The public inquiry report was published later that day and debated in the House of Commons.

Sir Desmond wrote a brief letter to Transport Secretary Paul Channon:

I was appointed by you on 23 November 1987 to hold a formal Investigation into the circumstances of the King's Cross Underground fire. I have completed the investigation and enclose my report.

The brevity of the letter was nothing compared to the detail that followed, which placed the blame for the fire squarely at the feet of London Underground. Despite calls from the opposition benches for his resignation, Paul Channon survived. He told the house, 'I have asked London Regional Transport to have all these recommendations dealt with promptly.'

The report was headline news in the next day's papers: 'Managers guilty on Tube fire,' said *The Guardian*; 'Tube Chiefs Blind to Safety, Channon orders shake-up,' was *The Times'* headline. Sir Desmond was scathing in his report, forthright in his criticism but widely praised for leaving no stone unturned. He accused London Underground of 'dangerous blinkered complacency'.

In 1989, Fennell was appointed chairman of the General Council of the Bar, and in 1990 was knighted and appointed to the High Court. He stood down after a year in office when he suffered a stroke at the age of 57, three years after his report was published.

The beautiful lounge in the retired judge's house was adorned with floral-patterned lampshades and curtains, and to the right of him was a dark-wood antique bureau. As I sat there I couldn't help wondering what might have become of Sir Desmond had he been able to continue with a career he was devoted to. There was a similarity with what had happened to both of us: career-minded public servants unexpectedly finding ourselves on another path. Despite his disability, despite the passing of 20 years, he hadn't lost any of his candour on hearing of ongoing communications problems.

'What did you think about the multiple suicide bombings in 2005 and the fact that King's Cross was involved again and that communication was raised as an issue?'

'Well...' He paused. 'Despair, really, because it meant a lot of the work I'd done and the recommendations I'd made had not been carried out. I was reasonably convinced at the end of the King's Cross fire inquiry that we had managed to crack the problems that had arisen. There was unanimity among all the parties to it that the recommendations be made. I prioritised what should be done first – I couldn't do more than that. Which were the most important and how and when? I was despondent about the 7/7 attacks; it meant none of the recommendations had been carried forward. I felt a sense of despair.'

'Why do you think there was a lack of will to make the issue of communication work?'

'London Underground were very complacent: about their position, their pre-eminence as the best, the biggest and the most experienced underground service in the world. There was absolutely no cross-fertilisation and they were convinced that what they did was automatically the best. They undoubtedly had safety enshrined in their ethos, but when you actually asked "what does that mean?" they merely said, everything we did was based on safety.'

In other words, London Underground was an organisation where workers stayed in jobs for a long time resisting change, and were astonished by the suggestion that they should take external advice on safety.

'Do you think something similar could happen again?'

'Well, I very much hope not. I haven't been around London Underground to see what they have done but I think they must have taken on-board a great deal of what was said. They were certainly willing to do so; it looked as though they were looking for a catalyst to put this into operation. They agreed to all the recommendations. These were drawn up and appeared in the public inquiry report itself.'

We headed back to London to interview Peter Power, a former police inspector who was on duty on the night of the fire, and Sophie Tarassenko, whose brother Ivan had perished. We'd spoken at length and she said she was worn down by requests every year to give more interviews. It was only because I'd been a firefighter that she agreed to do the interview, and we were really able to connect. She struggled to believe that communication between emergency service workers underground was still not possible 20 years after the King's Cross fire. We usually catch up every year now at the memorial at the train station – and that's all the reminder I need of how much worse off the families are compared to how I was left feeling. It struck me one year when she said her brother had now been dead longer than he'd been alive.

I found it inspiring that I was able to use my experience across two careers and was totally immersed in the story. Colleagues from local radio, national radio news, the BBC continuous news channel and the broadcaster's website were all getting more interested. It was the first time I'd ever gone back over an incident I'd been involved in with such forensic detail. The London Fire Brigade was criticised, but I knew from my research that new radios were on their way – both on the underground network and for the emergency services so they would be able to communicate between street level and below the ground.

Sir Desmond's comments about being able to put a man on the moon stayed with me. I was deep into the story, able to ask the questions I'd never have been able to ask as a firefighter. I felt driven to raise awareness on behalf of the loved ones of those who died at the fire.

It was a Thursday, three days before the 20th anniversary. I was briefing a news editor about the story when he interrupted.

'Why don't you do a "live", Clifford? On Sunday.'

'What you mean: come into the studio and talk about the anniversary?'

'Why not? You were on duty back then.'

'OK. I could talk about my recollections of that night, what's changed and what more needs to be done.'

'Good. Let's go and talk to Pete and get your details on the prospects.'

I'm usually quite happy working behind the camera. But an opportunity came my way to expand on the King's Cross fire in greater detail. I was excited, nervous, but most of all I was determined to get it right. Not for me, but for the victims and in the hope that my small journalistic contribution could accelerate change.

It was a rainy day, icy-cold too. The depressing grey weather fitted the mood of the moment. I drove up from Kent to London on the Saturday night. I'd written a backgrounder for the BBC website, and had a warm-up on Friday morning for my colleagues on local radio. My head was full of facts: Sir Desmond's 157 recommendations, the problems encountered during the 7 July attacks, the names and details of all the new communications equipment that was coming, and details of the pot of money from which the government was going to pay for it all.

I parked my car at BBC Television Centre, at the time the home of all UK news, and walked up the stairs. The presenter, Tim Willcox, was about to go on-air, and would be interviewing or two-waying me as we called it. We'd worked together before so we had a good rapport.

'Clifford! Good to see you. So you were a fireman? That's amazing.'

'Hi Tim. Yes, I was, and you know doing this means a lot to me.'

'For sure. We're going to do a really good job on this.'

Tim's approach was brilliant. I showed him a couple of photos of me in uniform, and we talked through the brief and the line of questions.

I was nervous. I'd done some reporting but felt a massive responsibility for what I was doing now. This wasn't about me but the victims and my former colleagues. My two careers were about to come together in a unique and unexpected way and my head was full of bullet points.

My interview with Sir Desmond had been woven into a videotaped report, pulled together by another colleague, reporter Graham Satchell, which we'd edited a couple of days before. The plan was that Tim would read the introduction to the report live, the short film would be played-out and I'd be sitting next to him for our two-way off the back.

I still had an hour to go, so I waited in the green room, which was actually an open balcony with some bucket seats, a pile of discarded scripts and some lukewarm coffee. I was going over the story in my head, rehearsing my answers, when a make-up designer walked on to the balcony and dusted my face.

Suddenly it was real. The years of suffering: Colin Townsley, Body 115, Ralph Humberstone – the families of all those people. I had to get it right for them.

'Mr Thompson?' It was the floor manager. 'It's OK. I work here. just call me Cliff or Clifford.'

'OK, Clifford, let's get you on set and mic'd up.'

I nodded to Tim who was shuffling his briefing notes.

'Stand by, Tim,' said the floor manager. He stood by the camera with the presenter's script on the autocue, the red light on the camera came on, and the floor manager flicked his hand in a sharp movement, cueing Tim to start reading, and the studio was live.

'It's 20 years since a fire that began on a wooden escalator ripped through King's Cross Underground station in London. The blaze killed 31 people and injured another 60. Since then new safety measures have been put in place, but the man who chaired the public inquiry into the disaster says some lessons have still to be learned.' Tim read the introduction with perfect ease, and for the next two-and-a-half minutes our news film played out.

The red light on the camera lit up again. Tim looked straight into the lens as the script on the autocue screen slowly inched up line by line.

'Well, with me now is BBC journalist Clifford Thompson, also a former Red Watch firefighter. Clifford, what are your memories of that day?'

I told how I'd been on duty with Red Watch colleagues at Stratford that day, and how we heard that a major incident had happened over the radio but hadn't been called in.

'Gradually the incident escalated. There were about 150 to 200 firefighters called on,' I explained. 'We were kept in our station. Then we heard the tragic news that Station Officer Colin Townsley had lost his life.'

My face flushed but I was through the first and most difficult question.

'And you subsequently formed part of the guard of honour?' Tim asked.

'We were actually posted right outside King's Cross station

for Colin's funeral. It was a very moving experience and there were thousands of firefighters from all over the UK – all over Europe, in fact, which was really surprising.'

'Interesting that, 20 years on, the fire service still hasn't got radios that work underground. Why has it taken so long?'

I explained how the fire service had invested in a brand-new system called Fire Link, which would be available in 2009 and able to patch into other emergency services so that they could talk to each other. Eventually they would also be able to talk to workers underground as well.

I was well into my stride, a wave of adrenaline washing over me, keeping me alert, focused and able to reel off my facts as Tim's questions kept coming.

'Isn't there anger in the fire service that it has taken 20 years for this to happen?'

'Sir Desmond Fennell made 157 separate recommendations. He was scathing about poor communications, the way the emergency services and London Underground work. There have been many practical changes now: for example, plans to all the tunnel networks are kept outside the stations, whereas at King's Cross they had been kept deep underground – completely in the wrong place.'

'And when you look at the equipment, that has changed radically too?'

'The changes to protective equipment came around pretty quickly after King's Cross. We used to wear what were known affectionately as "boil-in-the-bag" leggings or overtrousers – basically something only suitable for when you go sailing, which are now replaced with padded knees and Kevlar helmets. Some fire services use the Cromwell helmet, where the ears are completely enclosed.'

Tim asked what else still needed to be done, and I explained how the government had invested £56 million into the fire service for the provision of urban search-and-rescue equipment. This had been used recently in the summer flooding and to recover the bodies of three firefighters killed at the Warwickshire warehouse fire (a fourth died in hospital).

'So much has changed in 20 years. We didn't even have mobile phones. I can remember covering this as a newspaper journalist,' said Tim.

'Exactly. We were using field telephones and all sorts of kit that just didn't work together. There was no synergy. But the way the emergency services work with each other has improved.'

'Clifford, thanks very much for coming in to talk about the disaster 20 years ago.'

The weather forecast followed my interview, I got up left the studio and walked around to the newsroom.

'Well done, Clifford,' said one of the producers. 'We were cheering in the gallery for you – well done, mate. We'll probably clip it up and rerun it in the next hour.'

I walked out of the newsroom towards my car. It was raining – freezing cold. It was more than 15 years since I'd fought a fire, and my hope was that my research, my words, my explanation of what happened would make some impact.

I got into my car and drove straight to King's Cross Station.

Railway stations are funny places in as much as they evoke strong emotions in us: the wounded coming home from war, the lovers meeting on the platform, travellers seeking adventures. For me, the railway station is a place of atmosphere, tension and drama. The railway is so symbolic of communication, so central to our function, whether it's moving commuters, shifting freight – there's always a sense of urgency.

I parked a few streets away from the station and walked around icy puddles, and onto the slippery concourse. I stood there as I had at Spencer Park, absorbing the moment and trying to superimpose my memories of the tragic night over the bustle of those lugging backpacks, snatching hot coffees and scrutinising tickets.

I wondered how many people knew the significance of that station on that day: the fear and deep sadness that resonated for so many after lives had been destroyed. I walked down the steps from the Euston Road entrance into the subterranean maze in search of the memorial. For much of the past 15 years I'd shut out a considerable amount of what I'd seen as a fire-fighter. For a long time I never discussed my former career with other journalists.

At one end of a very long foot tunnel is the memorial to the fire. In fact, the station has two memorials. The victims are honoured by a large stone slab set into the wall of a foot tunnel, and a clock in the ticket hall. The 21st-century King's Cross has been rebuilt so not everything is exactly where it was in 1987. Underneath the stone were some flowers, placed there earlier in the day during a service of remembrance. I read through the list of 31 names. It felt strange as passengers weaved their way around me. I must have looked odd, fixed to the spot and deep in thought, contemplating what had gone before. I thought few people rarely go to a station to have a think about things. I was the only person not going to, or coming from, somewhere else. My journey was an emotional one.

On the drive home, a producer from one of the BBC's national radio networks called. She had seen me on television, and wanted to know if I could go back to the studios later that night to do an interview down-the-line with a presenter in

Manchester. I agreed and returned to work later that night with only a few hours of the anniversary remaining.

The fire in which Gordon died made me more spiritual. I never really thought about what happened to the people, or rather the souls of people, who lost their lives. Like many people I never imagined the process of dying, but was just aware that it could happen in the most bizarre ways, and when least expected. But today I think much more about what might happen. I like to believe that the spirit lives on, or returns to occupy a new body, so that our knowledge and experience is cumulative – although it probably sounds far-fetched to imagine a newborn baby coming into the world full of knowledge it can't yet articulate.

In my 20s I was more pre-occupied with the notion that death and dying were real. If we never think about it, or pre-pare emotionally for it, the impact is much worse when it happens unexpectedly. The shocking circumstances in which we often saw people brought home the reality of death, but I was still constantly frustrated by the question, 'Why?'

Firefighters I worked with often spoke about death in terms of 'moving on' or not getting 'too involved.' But when it came to the death of a child, I often heard it said, 'It always stays with you.'

Firefighters are trained to rescue people and protect prop-erty from destruction. No one wants to fail. During my time at training school we were tested with a new challenge every day. The biggest of these was an intense two-week breathing apparatus course which, if you failed, meant being pushed back to repeat the course, or possible dismissal. One of the toughest challenges I ever did was to enter a sewer pipe in the dark, wearing breathing apparatus that weighed around

30lbs. The diameter of the pipe was so small that it meant shuffling along on my knees with one arm ahead and one tucked behind. When I completed the test I knew my dream career was in sight, but there were still more barriers to clear during my first days after training school, when I was on probation.

Once posted to my station, there was more to come: the first fire in breathing apparatus, first stiff, first road-traffic collision, first major incident. But the fire in which Gordon died was too overwhelming and emotionally damaging. Had I fallen through a roof and shattered my thigh bone, everyone would understand; but a psychological wound was something of a taboo, a sign of weakness, and that equalled failure in the eyes of some. It took years for attitudes to change.

His death had forced me to retreat into myself, and as a consequence I didn't keep in touch with any of my former colleagues for many years. Straight afterwards I'd been on sick leave, so had no opportunity to talk about the events of that night with them. When I worked at the area HQ I was either alongside civilians or senior officers in a formal environment: not conducive to opening up. Instead I took it all away with me, which, I realise now, may have made it harder for me to recover.

Nor had I kept in contact with the vicar, Mervyn Popplestone. The last time we met was before Gordon's funeral, when he promised to send me 'something' while I was staying at my parents. Early in 1992, a letter and package containing a copy of The Living Bible, arrived in the post; it's paraphrased to make it easier to understand, written in plain English. I kept it in my bookcase, along with my children's Bible with its colourful pictures, but Mervyn's letter was packed away with all my notes, diaries and reports about the fire.

What I was most troubled about was the report about Gordon sent to the staff office on the night of the fire, which described him as dead-on-arrival at hospital. A decade after the fire, this still unsettled me, but I struggled to talk to anyone about it. I knew that Bill McGuyver, my station officer at Ilford, was also convinced Gordon had still been alive, and I remembered him telling me, 'It feels like a little bird fluttering – just keep going.' But if he was dead when he reached the hospital, it magnified my failure.

In September 2002, I had visited New York for a long weekend. On the Saturday, I met writer and psychologist Peter Micheels, who became a close friend after I interviewed him during my filming trip to the city in 1993. We were having lunch when we started to talk about the fire in which Gordon died. I'd never gone into detail with Peter, but he knew I'd served in the London Fire Brigade, and that I'd been involved in some challenging incidents.

'The hardest thing about that job was being convinced that the boy was alive, trying so hard to save him and losing the battle,' I said.

'Talk me through the events that led to his death,' Peter replied.

I told him how I'd laid out Gordon, who was unconscious, in the front garden, and blew into his mouth and over his nose. I remembered how his lungs had risen, and how he'd vomited when I picked him up and ran with him. Peter listened with just a slight movement of his head, a reassuring acknowledgement of what I was saying.

'I got him into a police car and a few minutes later he really began to vomit quite violently,' I continued.

I had never been able to talk about the detail of Gordon's final moments until now. 'It's OK,' Peter said, calmly. 'He was alive in order to vomit, because he was still able to gag,' he said. 'It's called the gag reflex, and he would have been alive to be able to do that.'

'But I heard from the coroner's report. I never saw it, but people told me that the coroner said he was dead in the fire.'

'The coroner wasn't there. *You were*. The coroner was wrong. The boy was alive.'

My eyes filled and my throat tightened. It was over a decade since Gordon died and in an instant I'd found some resolution in the most unlikely of sources.

We paid the bill, left the restaurant and took the subway to look at the remnants of the World Trade Center, now just a hole in the ground. A year earlier terrorists had succeeded at their second attempt to destroy it, and this time among the thousands who died were 343 New York firefighters. I paused in reflection, as I had at the King's Cross fire scene, on the day of Colin Townsley's funeral. But now I was just a civilian – no badge, no uniform or proof of my rescue credentials. It was a grey moment in bright sunlight. Although I wasn't wearing a uniform I raised my right arm in a smart naval salute; for Gordon, for the 343 heroes, for the thousands of victims; and for all those whose lives had briefly touched mine with such force.

We sat in a cab in silence as we rode uptown. Neither of us fancied the subway.

It was in 2004, when I was 37, that I decided to try and piece together my fragmented memories of the fire and Gordon's death. I was still troubled by the idea of what I didn't know about what happened that night. I wanted to pull all the facts together and get them all down on paper, to build a record of that night. I was still working on the BBC Breakfast programme, and had made a deal with myself that I was researching and exploring the events of that night as if it were a journalistic assignment. I hoped it would help me deal more with my feelings in a positive way. But I was soon to think differently.

I opened the box containing all my notes and diaries and took out Mervyn's letter:

6th January 1992

Dear Clifford,

We appreciate you attending our church and calling on me for prayer and blessing. Thank you for feeling that you could open your heart to me. I continue to pray for you.

You have passed through a very traumatic and draining experience. The answer to the question 'Why?' is something we will never fully know until we meet God. Even the great apostle Paul said, 'For now we see in a mirror dimly, but then face-to-face. Now I know in part; but then I shall understand fully... (I Corinthians 13:12)...

I cried as I read it. It was difficult to take in just how much of a mess I was in at the time. I was the rescuer who needed rescuing. I felt ashamed to talk about my problems, being psychologically damaged made me feel weak. But I will understand, I thought.

Generations before me had suffered worse through war and conflict, and it wasn't my child who died that night. It had been a lonely time, mute and isolated, in which the years of training and honing my skills of firemanship were lost.

Mervyn's letter went on to say that my experience would 'bring me closer to God, and open my heart to Jesus,' who would be my own 'personal saviour from sin, and, lord and master of your life.' Years later his words still resonated.

I opened my diary and read the entry for 20 December 1991. *Steve passed the baby to me and I began mouth-to-mouth resuscitation, etc.... took the baby to King George the Fifth [hospital] by police car.* I hadn't written that Gordon died in my arms or was dead on arrival at the accident department.

I got in my car and drove to Ilford in search of the house from which we rescued Gordon. I couldn't remember the address, although I had it in my notes. I just wanted to drive, alone, and relive that night. I got as far as Ilford town centre and turned around. I came home, boxed up the papers and put them in a cupboard.

I was upset and had strayed into an emotional disaster zone. The last thing I wanted was to get into a situation where I would need 'rescuing' again. It was too much. I couldn't face the prospect of going back to Eton Road or finding Gordon's mother, Kim. Even reading the slightest detail of the fire overwhelmed me.

It was a bad idea.

CHAPTER 12

The Search for Kim

I'm standing in the watch room. I'm carrying my fire boots and over-trousers, arranging my equipment on the back of the machine or up at the front, leading my crew. The rest of the firefighters are already on duty. I appear outside the station and ring the front doorbell. Then I'm in the front cab, pressing my foot on the button that sounds the sirens. It's real. There's a fire – and it's going like a bastard. I'm first in. All the old faces are there: Roger, Bert, Tom and tonight it's the big one...

I can't remember when the dream started. It has developed over time, from not being able to sleep after the death of Gordon, to the dream being a nightly event; sometimes it's weekly, or I can go for a month or so without it happening. It's always set in the same place: Stratford Fire Station, but in the here and now. Sometimes the dream extends into a bizarre fantasy where I'm being dropped into a major disaster by helicopter, to rescue people who have been severely burned, with thick layers of skin and flesh peeling back. When it comes to thinking about Gordon, some days I suffer, and some days I don't, but I've learned to cope – the dream continues.

While I was at Stratford we were called to a fire in a workshop in the middle of the day. A cylinder had exploded, engulfing a worker in flames. He staggered outside conscious, still on his feet but in deep shock. Large flakes of shrivelled skin were peeling from his badly burned arms, showing the glistening pink flesh underneath. In my complacency, such tragedies were filed away. Besides, something similar would always happen again soon after.

Years later, I believe my mind has converted the graphic detail of the terrible things I saw, into a sanitised version, something I can cope with. But I know my dream will happen, again and again. It takes me back to my younger self, a hero revelling in the glory and the tragedy, when I thought I could just carry on doing that job without anything changing.

About six months before I left the fire service and shortly after the fire in early 1992, Gordon's mother, Kim Taylor, visited area headquarters where I was working. The building was attached to the fire station and we stood at the front door. She brought Karl and Karlene with her and they gave me some home-made thank you cards for trying to save their brother. Kim asked me to be Karlene's godfather. I said no. I wanted to draw a line under the events that led to Gordon's death and I was leaving the fire service. I was coping much better with what had happened, and an outsider probably wouldn't have any idea, from looking at me, of what I'd been through. I was 25 and about to start again in a new career, without knowing what was ahead of me, without a job to go to. Kim said she was disappointed but that she understood. I felt I'd given a lot, and needed some distance from the fire and the family. I'd served for seven years. I was beaten.

After I left the fire service, I'd often wondered what had happened to Kim and the children – my suffering was tiny compared with her loss. I'd think about what it would be like if we met again. Things had changed; she wouldn't know I was no longer a firefighter. And with the passing of time I was able to talk about my experience without reliving the moment.

Covering the King's Cross anniversary had helped me and given me new confidence to try and find Kim. My last effort to do this in 2004 had failed because I hadn't been ready. What happened with Gordon still hung over my head, and my urge for a resolution grew. I felt I needed to go through the story of that terrible night one more time, and hear Kim's version of it.

Now it was six years later, the summer of 2010, as I gathered up journals, notebooks and photographs: anything that would remind me about my time as a firefighter and the events of nearly 20 years before. Had I coloured my own account of events? It was still so vivid in my mind, but perhaps I'd got it all wrong? I'd even forgotten the name of the road in which the fire happened.

I could either leave it as unfinished business, with the risk of never knowing what really happened that night, or rake it all up and expose myself to all the painful emotions again, making myself vulnerable. I decided it was time to take a journey back to Christmas 1991, now more determined than ever.

I started by searching for Kim on the Internet, going through the motions at first to see how I felt. I found nothing and was disappointed. I searched through some boxes and found my old fire service notebook, which confirmed the address as Eton Road. I also found the transcript of one of the reports filed on the night of the fire:

Tell the area commander that at the four-pump persons-reported fire, which occurred at 247 Eton Road Ilford, at 21:02 hours today 20/12/91, Gordon Taylor, aged three, was rescued from the front bedroom on the first floor by breathing apparatus crews and was certified dead-on-arrival at King George's Hospital. Junior Taylor aged 40, Kim Hamilton aged 29 and Karl Hamilton aged five, all suffered smoke inhalation and shock and all were removed to King George's Hospital and detained. A report will follow. Assistant Divisional Officer Boyes informed.

The report was distressing. Its tone was cold, written in the official style of the fire service; but it stated that Gordon was dead-on-arrival at the hospital. If I was going to move on and find Kim, I would have to find out whether to believe the report or my own instinct. The message was dictated to the staff office after the fire at 00:10. I turned to the report showing the timeline of events that night. The first informative radio message from the fire sent at around 21:10 said: *One child rescued from first-floor level, suffering from smoke inhalation, attempts being made to resuscitate.* We worked on Gordon for eight minutes until Station Officer McGuyver ordered me to remove him in the police car.

The 'stop' message sent from the fire ground by radio was 35 minutes later at 21:45, but it makes no mention of Gordon being dead at the fire: *one boy rescued from first floor, via internal staircase by BA crew, burned, overcome removed by police vehicle...* The use of the word 'overcome' confirmed my belief that senior officers assessing the fire from the outside also thought Gordon was alive. It was reassuring, but the incident timeline conveyed enough of the drama to upset me and tears flowed.

The term 'dead-on-arrival' appears to have no precise definition. So it's possible that Gordon died at any point from being caught in the fire to his arrival at the hospital with me to be classified as such. From the time he was rescued to his death being pronounced, Gordon received continuous first aid. Removing him in a police car was not going to give him the same level of medical care that would have been provided by an ambulance crew or doctor at the scene, but he was looked after. I was sure that Gordon was alive when he was pulled from the fire. I went with my gut feeling, reinforced by the conversation with Peter Micheels in New York, about a body being alive in order to have a gag reflex.

I read through all the reports and notes several times. It was the best form of therapy because the more I read, the easier it became to understand and I felt more calm. If I was going to find Kim, I was determined to have as many of the facts to hand as possible. I didn't want her to see me upset.

I wanted to know exactly when Gordon died, although it was clear that this was going to be impossible to determine. But I was sure that Gordon was alive when he was handed to me at the bottom of the stairs. At the time, Station Officer McGuyver agreed with me that there was a pulse, 'like a little bird fluttering'. When I shone my torch into his eyes, he didn't look dead but unconscious. In my report filed straight after the incident I wrote: *While carrying out CPR at the scene, I examined Gordon Taylor's eyes; they did not respond to my torchlight, however a faint and rapid pulse was detected at the boy's wrist.*

I remembered his chest rising and falling as I breathed into his mouth. I remember the force with which he vomited over my face as I ran, clutching his body, which could have been caused by his airway clearing or the final stage of his life. I looked again at Mervyn Popplestone's letter: 'The answer to the question "why?" is something we will never fully know.' I was preparing to uncover the past, but I also expecting disappointment. I would probably never know 'why?' so I put the question out of my head. Trying to put to rest the awful events of that night became my aim.

It was a weekday in August when, as if preparing for an expedition across a wild emotional landscape, I made a flask of tea and pulled on my hiking boots and a fleece. My first stop was Ilford and the scene of the fire. I drove past the fire station, and followed the route we took that night: right, right again, into Eton Road. As I drove I remembered picking up the radio handset: *F-E, Foxtrot four-two-one, Foxtrot four-two-two...*

status three... I was going back in time, on a trip to a museum containing the relics of my life.

It was a muggy day, blooming clouds hung heavy in the air and I stopped my car well short of the house. I got out of the car and walked slowly towards number 247. The house looked the same. A bit tatty, but it was clearly occupied. I wondered what the chances were of Kim still living there. The road was quiet – too quiet. No children playing out, few cars, but then four people smartly dressed came walking along the road, knocking on doors, so I stood where I was just outside the house. I realised then that they would reach 247 in a few moments. A man in a suit walked up to the door while curtains twitched.

'My friend, you look lost,' he said. 'Will you come with us for spiritual guidance? Come and find the Lord.'

I didn't reply but watched as one of his fellow disciples knocked on the door of 247 – it was opened by a black girl, about eight, with her hair in small bunches.

It's Karlene, I thought – Gordon's sister, and I stopped myself from crying out, my heart thumping. Then I remembered that Karlene was about eight at the time of the fire, so she'd be 28 now: I was being ridiculous. The group continued and once they were out of sight, I walked up and down, close to the house several times. A bin across the road had been emptied onto the pavement; there was an odd shoe and a chicken carcass. I felt self-conscious but I couldn't help stopping to examine the now-cracked crazy paving where I'd carefully laid out Gordon's body.

Take him in the police car, Cliff – just go...

I couldn't bring myself to knock on the door. What would I say? I felt as though I was doing something wrong. I'd seen the memorial to the lives lost at King's Cross, but there was no memorial for Gordon: the street kept his death a secret.

I returned to my car and drove to the offices of the local newspaper, opposite Ilford Fire Station. I walked into the reception, a woman barely looked up from behind a counter as I showed her my press pass.

'I wonder if you could help me? I'm trying to find out more about a story you covered–'

'When was it?' she interrupted.

'It was 1991–'

'We only keep recent stuff, from the past year here.'

'It's a story about a boy who died in a fire –'

'Yes, but we don't have all those newspapers here. They'd fill this whole building. Can you imagine? You'll have to go to the British Library.'

Her impatience and patronising attitude sparked something in me. I was going to find out about Kim and her family one way or another, and I suddenly felt even more motivated by her rudeness.

I drove to Leytonstone, to St Patrick's cemetery, and although I'd felt uneasy about visiting the house, I felt even more uneasy about going to the cemetery. But this is where I'd find Gordon's memorial. Boosted by the intransigent attitude of the receptionist at the newspaper, I parked my car on an access road that went around the outside of the cemetery's grounds to set off on a much harder walk. The spot where Gordon was buried was not immediately obvious. All I could remember of New Year's Eve 1991 was the cold, the fading light and the sobbing punctuated by the vicar's words: *Unto Almighty God we commend the soul of our brother departed, and we commit his body to the ground; earth to earth, ashes to ashes, dust to dust; in sure and certain hope of the Resurrection unto eternal life...* I had a feeling where the grave would be, but decided to make a systematic sweep from one end to the other until I found the spot.

I walked through row after row of graves with old headstones from 1876; name after name, the same words regularly repeated: 'love', 'peace', 'no longer with us', and 'never forgotten'. There were a few people placing flowers on the graves. Then I came across a row of smaller headstones, there were teddy bears and toys, brighter colours pictures of young, smiling faces. I was in the children's area of the cemetery. I checked every row of graves – some twice, I must be close to Gordon's now. Nothing.

I didn't want anyone to know what I was doing so I hadn't asked about his grave in the superintendent's office when I first arrived. I treated it like a journalistic investigation, but I still felt a little uncomfortable. I hadn't really thought that maybe there was a record somewhere in an office of Gordon's burial. I spent about 90 minutes scouring the cemetery. The clouds sagged even lower, the sky threatening to burst as Central Line Tube trains rumbled above ground along one edge of the graveyard.

I walked into the office by the main gate. It was dark inside, with a counter and a small office next to it. A young man appeared, wearing a sweatshirt, jogging bottoms and trainers; it didn't really look like the uniform of a cemetery superintendent and I was shocked by his informality.

'I wonder if you could help me, please? I'm trying to find out about a funeral that took place here on the 31st December 1991.'

'Not a problem, sir. I'll get the book.' He went into a storeroom and quickly re-appeared with a large black leather bound ledger.

'What date did you say?' He dropped the ledger on to the

counter with a crash and dust flew up filling the room. My notebook was concealed – tucked into my pocket.

'December 31st – Gordon Taylor.'

He opened the ledger, and ran his left forefinger down a column. 'There you go, final entry in the book, the last funeral of 1991, page 263.'

I stared at the ledger, Gordon's details were beautifully written by a calligrapher, and now there was some tangible evidence and small reference to his short life and my past.

The entry read: *31/12/1991, 384A, Gordon Taylor, 3. 371 Upton Lane E7, Grave 22, 17A, cash received £35. Ceremony performed by...* It wasn't possible to read the vicar's name.

'I'd like to see his grave.'

'Look, I tell you what, sir. I've got to go and see one of the gravediggers over the far side of the cemetery. I'll write the plot details on this card, but I'll walk over with you too, and show you where it is.'

'Thank you. Thank you very much.'

He pulled out a very small old-fashioned postcard. In small print at the top were the words, *Have pity on me, at least you, my friends, for the hand of the Lord hath touched me.* Then: *St Patrick's, the only Catholic cemetery in the East of London.* To the right of that were the opening times and then on the lower left the words 'grave', 'section' and 'row', by which the superintendent copied the details from the ledger to the card: grave 22, row 17, plot A.

As we walked I couldn't think of what to say to him. I was preparing myself to be asked who I was and what I was doing. He said nothing so we just walked at a brisk pace in silence.

'There you are, sir. It's here somewhere – between these two.' He counted the rows of graves. 'Fourteen, 15, 16, 17... 22's about here – yes: plot "A".'

'What do you mean "somewhere here"? Is there no headstone?'

'Well, it looks that way to me.'

'You mean you can just bury a child and there's no grave, no headstone, nothing to show where they're buried?'

'That's right, sir. The cemetery is laid on a grid so we can find where every burial was.'

'Please, can I go back to the office and look at the book? I just want to spend a few minutes here first.'

'That's fine, sir, I'll be over there for a bit but I've left it out. Just go in the office and help yourself. I'll leave you to it.'

At my feet was a bare patch of new grass that was finer and greener than the surrounding area. I stood looking at the ground under a weighty sky. It didn't feel like the same place I'd stood in 1991, the place where I helped cover the grave with soil, where I left a cap badge for Gordon. I remembered the vicar's words: *In sure and certain hope of the resurrection to eternal life through our Lord Jesus Christ, we commend to Almighty God our brother, Gordon...*

I felt angry at first that he didn't have a headstone – it suggested that he had been forgotten about, and the thought upset me. I imagined it was impossible that anyone, particularly a child, could be buried without any kind of memorial, or marker. It was a warm, bright day compared with that last cold, grey day of 1991. I was in a much better place now, I wasn't hurting as much, but being there still stirred me and I didn't find it easy.

I bent over and brushed my fingers through the soft grass and disturbed a small downy feather, then I went back to the office and studied the ledger. I looked at the address in Upton Lane, in Forest Gate – it wasn't Kim's address in Ilford, and it wasn't the tower block where I visited Kim and Reggie between the fire and the funeral. I left the cemetery clutching my notebook and the card that had the details of Gordon's plot. It only took about 20 minutes to reach the house. I pulled up nearby in a side road. Something came over me – I knew that if I didn't act immediately, I never would. Without hesitating I walked straight up to the front door and rang the bell. A black lady answered the door.

'I'm sorry to trouble you,' I said, and took out my press pass trying to formulate the words in my head. She looked at me, her eyebrows raised in anticipation as I held up the pass, so that even if she thought my sudden appearance on her doorstep was odd, she'd have proof of my name. 'I wonder if you can help me, please? I used to be a firefighter, I'm now a journalist, but a long time ago I was involved in a fire where a young child died. I've just come across your address and wondered if you knew what happened to Betty Hamilton or Kim Taylor?'

'Yes, I know Betty very well. She's my friend and we did a house swap.'

'You mean you're still in touch with them?'

'Yes. I haven't seen Betty for a while, but she lived here when that tragedy happened. Shocking.'

'Could you contact her for me please?'

'Yes, of course.'

'Can you give me a moment?' I said, 'I'd like to leave a note with my number.'

'OK, I'll be here. Give me another knock.'

I walked back to my car. I couldn't believe that I'd found a link to Betty. I felt nervous but excited, I picked up my notebook from the back seat of my car and wrote:

Dear Betty and Kim, I hope you are both well. I was wondering if you remember me? My name is Clifford Thompson. I was one of the fire-fighters involved in the rescue of Gordon. I'd love to speak to you as I'm writing about my experience as a firefighter. It would be great to speak to you both.'

I signed the impromptu letter filled out on a lined page of my reporter's notebook and went back to the house, knocked again and handed it to the lady.

It had been an extraordinary day, and as I drove off, I wondered what would happen if Betty or Kim called; maybe neither would. Perhaps it was a chapter in their lives that was closed for good and they resented me for what happened. Or they thought I was no longer a hero. But for the time being there was not much more I could do other than wait.

In one day, I'd been back to Eton Road for the first time, found Gordon's burial plot and a link to his family. It made me realise that memorials, graves, tangible reminders of those lost, were so important. Disasters throw people into extreme and unexpected situations; the victims sometimes subsequently deny them, refuse to mourn, and avoid memorial services which I believe could hinder the recovery of the victims.

Of course I didn't suffer in any way that began to come close to Gordon's family, but the ripple of a disaster carries its consequences for many people. It might have been wrong in some people's eyes for me to get so involved, both at the time and by revisiting Gordon's story 20 years later. But the talking, the reflection and research had strengthened my understanding.

I gazed over the view from High Beach in Epping Forest. It

was much brighter than it had been earlier that day when I was at Eton Road and the cemetery. It was quiet, then my phone rang.

'Is that Clifford?'

'Yes. Can I help you?' It was a woman, her voice sounded elderly and shaky.

'It's Betty – Betty Hamilton. How are you Clifford?'

'Oh Betty. It's great to hear from you. I can't believe it. How are you? I'm fine, I'm not in the brigade anymore, but how are you – you and Kim?'

'Clifford, we're fine, we're OK – all this time, we were wondering what happened to you.'

'Well, I'm OK. I've moved on – I'm not in the fire service any more, but I'd really like to talk to you and Kim sometime. Would that be possible?'

'Of course you can. You spoke to Tina, my friend. She called me straight away to tell me about the note and give me your number. We've often wondered what had happened to you. We were so proud of you for everything you did. It meant so much to us all.'

'It was important for me to be at the funeral,' I said.

'You were very emotional. You told us, "I thought I had him. I just thought I had him".'

We agreed to meet in a couple of weeks. That conversation with Betty made all my efforts to find the family worth it.

CHAPTER 13

The Meeting

It was a warm day in September 2010, and the low sun shone hazy rays. I arrived at the coffee shop in Leytonstone High Road early and reserved a table on the first floor, which would give us a bit more privacy.

I was determined to look smart so wore a grey suit that made me feel confident. I hoped after all these years that Betty and Kim were alright.

I ordered a coffee and they walked through the door. Kim was wrestling a pushchair, carrying her granddaughter up the steps, her handbag resting on top while Betty cleared a path to the counter. They didn't recognise me at first.

'Betty, Kim – hello,' I said.

'Clifford, how are you?' asked Betty.

'I'm fine. Good to see you. Thanks for coming.' There was a polite embrace.

'Hello, Clifford,' said Kim smiling. 'Remember Karl? Look here's his picture.'

We were a tangle of coffee cups, handbags, notebooks, my pocket recorder and Kim's pictures. I remembered Karl at the wake after Gordon's funeral, and when he came with Kim to see me at the fire station. Kim stuffed the picture of Karl's grown-up face beaming with a smile back into her bag. I wondered why she'd been so keen to show it to me. I ordered them both drinks but they refused anything to eat.

The Meeting

'I've got a table upstairs. Let's go: it's quieter there.'

Kim looked exactly the same as I remembered her, except now she was wearing glasses. The ice was broken and it was a happy moment.

'You remember Karl?' Kim asked again.

'Yes, he was rescued from the fire too, after Gordon, I think. I remember talking to him at your house.' Karl was brought to King George's Hospital on the night of the fire in the ambulance that eventually turned up, with Kim. He was five at the time – two years older than Gordon.

'We lost him too. He was stabbed to death in 2004.'

I realised now why Kim had been so keen to thrust the picture of him into my hand a few minutes earlier. I was stunned.

'Kim, I'm so sorry to hear that...'

'It's OK. I don't mind talking about it.' It put the whole moment under a cloud. Kim's suffering had doubled, but her face was a mask of composure.

'I'm happy to talk,' said Kim. 'We feel that if anything can be learned by what happened to Gordon... We want to tell you everything.'

I told them how I'd changed career, as a result of the fire, and how I'd been over the events of that night countless times. Kim also told me that she'd tried to find me on several occasions, which I found touching. This was the first time I'd heard the story of that night from anyone else. I was ready for Kim's account, but felt unsettled to hear of Karl's death.

'I want you to go back to that time and tell me about the day Gordon died.'

'We'd left mum's about 10 o'clock that night in a cab. Gordon had been to a party at nursery for Christmas – Santa had visited and given him a present. When we first got home he put it under the tree. He was going to leave it for Christmas, then he decided he wanted to open it. It was a farm set, with little animals and a plastic fence. Gordon and Karl were saying they were hungry, so I went in the kitchen and made them something to eat. After they ate Gordon asked, "Can I play upstairs?" and off he went with Karl.'

I remembered the excitement of my own childhood Christmases, going to bed on Christmas Eve and hoping my empty pillowcase would be full in the morning.

'The previous evening Gordon had been sick," Kim continued. 'But he insisted he was alright. I guess he was excited about Father Christmas. After they went upstairs to play, I must have dozed off on the sofa. The next thing I knew Karl came running downstairs saying, "Mum, there's a fire!" I can only describe it like being drunk, and suddenly sobering up in a second. I flew upstairs with Reggie behind me, as we looked in all the rooms. Reggie concentrated on the bedroom where the fire was, trying to get in. I opened all the wardrobes...' Kim's voice cracked, but she was determined to keep talking. Betty leaned forward.

I told Kim to take her time, and that she could stop at any point, but wondered whether Gordon's illness the day before could have been a factor in his death?

Before the meeting, I'd gone to the British Library to search for articles about the fire. A neighbour, William Gardiner, told the Ilford Recorder that he stepped outside and saw flames. He ran back to his house and told his wife to call 999, then tried to enter 247. 'The smoke was dense and acrid and pushed me back – three times I tried to get to the bedroom. I crawled along the floor and when I got to the door, a burst of flames hit me in the face.' I decided it was unlikely that Gordon's illness had contributed to his death, given that a grown man was unable to cope with the toxic fumes and intense heat.

Kim continued. 'I went in the bathroom, calling him but he wouldn't answer me. I can't remember if I was dragged out by one of your colleagues or a police officer. But I know eventually myself and Reggie were pulled out. The first thing I did was put Karl out on the street. He was so little.'

Although her voice was shaky, Kim kept her composure. I was intrigued by her account, but didn't recall seeing Karl outside the house at the time.

'The last thing I remember on the night was when I saw Gordon wrapped in the quilt when you were resuscitating him. In all the confusion I heard the ambulance was going to be 40 minutes and that's when you got into the back of the police car with him. Then an ambulance turned up and they put myself and Karl in it. There was a police officer with us, and Reggie was angry, blaming me and Karl for what had happened.' Although Kim had retold the story very quickly, so far events were exactly as I remembered them. The only difference was that she'd said she'd arrived home at 10pm that night, whereas the mobilising call into Ilford fire station was at 21:02.

'When we got to hospital it seemed like hours before they came and told us that he wasn't with us no more.'

I didn't see Kim, Reggie and Karl arrive at King George V hospital and I wasn't present when they were told Gordon had died.

'It seemed like forever, it really did – I know it wasn't but that's how it felt,' she said.

She fussed over the baby, who was just a couple of months old, looking down at her making cooing noises. It seemed strange to think that she was now a grandmother. It seemed as if the baby helped her remain calm and focused.

I asked Kim about how the fire started.

'First I thought it was my cigarette lighter that started it. Then I realised... well you think toddlers can't climb high, but you'd be surprised. The spare lighter was in the top kitchen cupboard... you'd have to climb on to the side to reach it. I knew Gordon was too short to reach the lighter, and that Karl must have got it, but I never blamed him.'

Kim's revelation that she thought Karl was responsible for starting the fire was a devastating moment. Her eyes darted nervously around the room as she spoke. 'Karl used to blame himself a lot for Gordon's death. But I used to tell him it wasn't his fault; it was just a game that went wrong.'

'In the police statement, they said Gordon was found on my bed under the quilt.

'The fire started in the little box room, but they went into my bedroom. They said Gordon and Karl flicked the lighter and it made them jump – then it sparked, and the mattress flared up. Karl panicked and came to get me.'

Again my memory was right. I remember standing at the top of the stairs that night. Through the smoke I could see the glowing fire in one room to my left, and Steve emerging with Gordon from another. Karl must have already been outside the house having gone to attract Kim's attention. 'I remember we found Gordon in one of the front bedrooms...' I said.

Kim replied, 'They always had to be together, naughty or good they were typical brothers.'

I was renting the property on a temporary basis and we'd only been there a few months.'

'What did you think of the fire crews?' I asked.

'I can always see you,' said Kim, 'I've never forgotten. I can always remember you and your colleagues pulling-up, how you rushed in with no mask when you heard Gordon was in there. The last vision I have is of him wrapped in a quilt as you tried to resuscitate him. That was the last time I saw him until the hospital, after he'd passed away. I didn't believe he was gone. I feared he would be severely burned, I didn't think he would die.'

As I listened to her version of events, it was like I was pulling an index card from my mental filing system, rereading it, correcting it and tidying it up before putting it away again.

I also felt reassured that Kim didn't have any criticism of my actions on that night. This was also the first time I'd ever spoken so intimately to a fire victim from a job I'd been involved in. She also didn't mind that I'd turned down her request to be Karl's godfather all those years ago.

'I could hear screaming as we jumped off the trucks,' I told her. 'It still haunts me.'

'The police put me in a house across the road. There were two officers by the door trying to stop me from coming out,' she recalled. 'I don't know where I got the strength from, but I remember pushing them out of the way and running across the road and seeing you with Gordon in the front garden. I remember sitting on the pavement outside. I must have wet myself about a dozen times in a minute or so. I remember putting my feet against the wall and it just collapsed.'

Kim's description of her rage, being able to force her way past the police officers and pushing the wall over was typical of the flood of adrenaline that can give both victim and rescuer superhuman strength. The screams were so loud, it was as if Kim and Reggie were directly behind me. It was another vivid and painful legacy of that night that has never lost its intensity whenever I think back.

Kim's voice quietened, and for the first time she sounded

bitter and exasperated. 'I always felt that if there wasn't a delay with the ambulance he would have pulled through. I truly believe that. I know you did everything you could. I have no problems with what you did. He just didn't make it. But I honestly think that if the ambulance had been there with oxygen, he'd be here today.'

'What was it like at the hospital? How did they tell you?' I asked.

'There was a nurse, a doctor and somebody else – three of them. They said, "We need to talk to you, take a seat, have a cup of tea." I said, "No. I want to see my baby. Whatever it is, just tell me." It was the doctor who said, "We're so sorry; we did everything we could but he's gone." I turned to Reggie and screamed, "He's gone! He's dead! He's dead!" They put him in a section and pulled the curtains round. We saw him laid on a trolley. There was a sheet up to his neck, they hadn't covered his face. He wasn't badly burned. He'd been killed by smoke inhalation.'

She told me that Gordon's death was recorded by the coroner as an accident, with smoke inhalation as the cause of death. It didn't feel like the right time for me to explore exactly when the coroner thought Gordon died. I also wanted to continue to believe that he was alive when I was resuscitating him.

Her voice softened as she remembered the son she'd lost. 'He was a very loving boy. Women would look at him and say, "He's gorgeous," and Gordon would go up to them and give them a kiss and cuddle. He'd kiss anyone.'

I asked if she'd ever gone back to the house.

'Reggie went back and salvaged what he could. I could never go back there. In fact, I've never been to Ilford since; it's nearly 19 years. Afterwards? It was day-by-day. The hardest thing was Christmas Eve...' Kim began to sob. 'We went to my mum's house and all the presents were there – for Karlene and Karl, as well as Gordon's presents with his name on, wrapped up. We used to put them on their bed. Christmas Day was horrible, but we tried our best, thanks to my mum, dad and nan.'

The mood lightened as suddenly Kim laughed, as she remembered the bed piled high with presents, saying Betty always bought the children's presents early, and how she did the same for her when she was a little girl.

The afternoon faded into early evening as the café bustled with customers oblivious to the loss the two women had suffered. Their bond was strong and they chatted like best friends. Kim talked about her grandmother, who was still alive in 1991, and how she was now a grandmother herself.

Their closeness and intimacy made me feel a little isolated and awkward. Despite coming from a close family – my parents had celebrated 50 years of marriage in 2009 – I hadn't married or had children. I was still drifting in and out of relationships, which troubled me as marriage is a strong institution in my family. My life had been one long ride through turbulence and when I was being realistic, I'd accept there was no chance of having kids of my own.

Kim still sees Reggie – they were separated at the time of the fire, but kept getting back together again – and explained that he never really knew what it was like to have a family around him. 'He didn't feel the same closeness as I did. He has not been fortunate to have a family.'

Kim now worked in a factory, Betty was a catering assistant at the Royal London Hospital and Reggie was a refuse collector. I wanted to know if Kim and Reggie were still in a relationship – Reggie was 40 at the time of the fire, so he'd be nearly 60 now. But I felt like I was intruding too much. But Kim said she'd told him we were meeting, and that he said 'Hello'.

As we chatted, it became clear just how extraordinary – and tragic – Kim's life had been. Before the fire she'd had a miscarriage, followed by another one. She then had her daughter, Kristina, who was 17, and the baby's mother; followed by another daughter, Kirsty, who had died from an asthma attack 10 months after Karl was murdered. Her eldest daughter, Karlene, was now 26 and suffered from depression.

'What happened to Karl?' I asked.

'He was stabbed several times.' Kim paused. 'It was in 2004. He'd taken four days off work and went to a nightclub for the first time in his life, then had gone on to play snooker. At six o'clock in the morning, the police came and said "There's been an incident with Karl."'

Much later I found a story written by the Press Association in September of the same year, during the trial of a 19-year-old man and 17-year-old youth, for his murder. The headline was 'Boy murdered in £15 drug debt' It described how a row 'led to a teenager being beaten and stabbed to death by a gang of youths in a street battle, the Old Bailey heard today... Karl Hamilton, 17, died from multiple stab wounds after he was surrounded, kicked in the head, beaten and stabbed repeatedly.'

Mohammed Miah, from Bethnal Green, East London, and the 17-year-old youth (who was not named for legal reasons) were cleared of Karl's murder. Even if I'd known this before I met Kim, I could never imagine asking her if Karl had been involved with drugs or gangs. It felt far too intrusive.

The Meeting

Kim took out the photo of her oldest son again.

'He would have loved to have met you.'

I found it hard to comprehend how Kim must have felt losing two sons in such awful circumstances, and I was shocked by the news that Kirsty had died.

'How do you feel about what's happened to you?'

'Nobody is a perfect person.'

But it was clear she didn't want to dwell on the deaths of her children, and instead told me about the day Gordon was buried.

'I went to the funeral directors in Plaistow every day. They were determined to hold the funeral between Christmas and New Year. I thought at first they just wanted to get rid of him, but they said wanted to end the year with the bad, and start the new year afresh.'

I was a little upset that she may not have had enough time to fully comprehend the extent of her loss before Gordon was buried.

'I remember seeing you at the gate as we arrived, all dressed up and you saluted Gordon. You did that for my son. It was more than I ever expected.' I felt moved by the affection and pride in her voice. 'It meant so much to the family, not just myself. Karl and Karlene were not at the funeral – they were too young. But it was all a blur, really.'

It felt too insensitive to mention Gordon's plot in the cemetery without a headstone, but I also wondered if Kim ever went to visit the grave.

'I was trying to find Gordon's plot. I went to the office...'

'I go the cemetery regularly, but Mum doesn't like going,' interrupted Kim. 'I go at least eight to 10 times a year. Unfortunately, I couldn't afford a headstone, but there should be plants there.' She'd answered the question I'd been too nervous to ask.

'How do you get over something like this?' I asked her.

'You don't. It's always there. Even now you have good days and bad days. I prefer to talk. Reggie won't.'

We took a break and had another drink, then Betty told me her version of events, and how she'd been looking after Gordon on the day of the fire.

'We were standing outside my doctor's playing a game of catch the moon behind the clouds; Gordon told me he was going to the moon, and all of a sudden a sheet of glass came from the second floor of a house and crashed to the ground. It was like some kind of warning. That night I got a call to say there was a fire, so I got a cab and rushed straight to the hospital.'

She recalled with clarity, confidence and dignity how she arrived at the hospital and demanded to see her grandson.

'A nurse said, "Wait inside and someone will come and talk to you," and I turned and walked out... I knew he'd gone. I went outside and banged my head against the wall.'

I remembered leaving the hospital that night and seeing Betty outside and alone, in tears. One of the most distressing things about that night was that image of Betty in her grief with no one to take her home, and how guilty I felt walking away.

Betty said her husband was determined that Gordon would return to their house before the funeral. 'The boy came home the night before we buried him. We had the coffin open, and apart from a slight burn on his chest, you wouldn't know he'd been in a fire. I said "Good night, God bless" to him. The next day, I remember seeing you at the funeral. Everyone thinks that firefighters, ambulance staff and nurses don't have feelings – but you proved that you do, and you gave so much comfort.'

I explained that the hardest thing for me had been seeing her at the hospital, distressed, and having to walk away.

'It shouldn't have happened,' said Betty. 'Gordon had a wonderful life but as my mother used to say, "He was too good for this world. He wasn't meant to be here." And I have to believe that for my own comfort, otherwise I'd go mad.'

I was amazed that the two women were able to tell their stories with such candour, and couldn't imagine how they were able to carry on with life without crumbling. My bravery was nothing compared to Betty and Kim's, it was just a thin veneer, but theirs was like solid wood, their courage running deep through the grain.

'How did you feel burying your grandson on New Year's Eve at the end of the year?' I asked.

'It's never a good time whenever it is. You've got to leave him in that cold ground; that's what hit me,' replied Betty.

'How have you kept your strength up for Kim?'

'I had a strong husband, and I had my mum, bless her, and my daughters. You keep going; you've got to – kids are a gift. You know you've got to keep strong for them, so you do your crying on your own. I still miss him, and wonder what he'd be doing now, where he'd be working. You imagine what it would be like.'

Then Kim turned the spotlight on me, and I felt over-whelmed by her words.

'I'm so pleased to meet you. It's been something I've wanted to do for many years, to thank you for what you did. We know you did more than you could – and our family will be eternally grateful.'

The moment was broken by sirens from noisy fire trucks

passing the café.

I explained how I hadn't been able to talk about it for a long time, and asked what kept her going.

'My mum, my daughters, my granddaughter… my job has been a big help. I used to spend a lot of time just in bed, but even after all these years, it sticks in your mind. I just take each day as it comes. It never goes away. It's always in my head and my heart.'

The meeting with Kim and Betty resolved many issues for me, and helped corroborate my account of events. For that alone I was grateful.

I waited for a few minutes after they left the café. I sipped the last of my coffee, stood up and walked through the front door. It was rush hour; the high road was busy with traffic. It was a warm and bright evening, greengrocers' shops displayed bowls of shining fruit on counters in the street; two children whizzed by on scooters, and a group of men, still in their work clothes, eagerly pushed open the door of the Red Lion pub. I stepped onto the pavement, looked down at my shoes, then up, and crossed the road alone, absorbed in my thoughts.

Epilogue

Writing this book has helped me come to terms with my time as a firefighter and crucially, has forced me to pick over events in forensic detail and broaden my understanding. Databases, the Internet, picture archives and social media have all allowed me to reconstruct events, and hear again some of the stories. Hopefully, in some small way, I'm providing my own archive of that time. Making contact with Kim and Betty was especially useful for two reasons: they still hold me in the highest regard for trying to save Gordon. It was always my fear that they'd somehow blame me for his death and not want anything to do with me. But it was also reassuring to know that our stories checked out – we agreed on many of the facts surrounding the events of that night. Before I met them, I felt that my own view of events was somewhat cloudy. But both Betty and Kim's accounts of that night add so much more to this story.

But it still took me until 2008 to set foot on a London fire station again, and that was just to buy a ticket for a retirement function for a former colleague. It was only in 2011 that I went back to Stratford to meet the Red Watch at the time. I have never been back to Ilford Fire Station, although I've driven past a few times. It's not something I've ever wanted to do, even though I was able to go back and find Gordon's house. The fire station, in emotional terms, is just too big, too meaningful. It keeps hostage everything that could trigger a reminder of the events of that terrible night and my career.

On a broader scale, writing and recalling my experiences have given me the chance to reflect on them and understand how they have shaped the person I am today.

What happened to me as a firefighter seems such a long time ago now, but I've been able to create a new life, even if it has sometimes been difficult to escape the past. I played a very small part in all the tragedies I dealt with, but I sometimes wish I could have served my 30 years as a firefighter, and I've begun to think about that more now I'm at the age I might have retired.

But I made a useful contribution. People often ask me how long I served, and when I say seven years they invariably say that it's a long time, even though it's much less than the 30 years I might have completed. Nowadays, firefighters are required to work until they are 60 after changes to their pension scheme a few years ago, but the job becomes much harder with age. It's physically and emotionally demanding and recent research has suggested that, apart from stress, firefighters are at greater risk of heart problems and cancer.

In the years since Gordon's death, I've realised that as I became more addicted to my job, I was simultaneously growing more vulnerable. I knew firefighters who had served 30 years at busy stations; some were affected by alcohol, or unable to stay in a stable relationship; the careers of others ended prematurely because of injuries that disabled them – either physical, psychological, or both. For some it's much worse. In 2008, I took a call one evening from a former colleague. It was to tell me that a firefighter we'd both worked with had taken his life. He walked out into the garden, entered the shed and blew his head off with a shotgun.

Epilogue

Today I think of those suffering alone and in silence.

But things have improved. Men are generally encouraged to talk more about their feelings, and to seek help. More information is available to firefighters about dealing with trauma, but crucially, more firefighters are willing to talk publicly about their experiences. The Fire Brigades Union has continued to campaign tirelessly for better working conditions, but social media has also played a major role. There are Facebook groups for serving and retired firefighters; there's a campaign by a mental health charity; Mind Blue Light, it even has its own Twitter page offering support and advice for emergency workers. For decades, The Fire Fighters Charity has been providing respite, recovery and physical training programmes for injured firefighters, and they now include some counselling sessions to serving and former firefighters, and fire and rescue services offer more counselling, and de-brief crews very soon after an incident – in some cases before they leave.

In my day, there was no Internet, there was no quick way of getting help or information although the brigade did have a welfare department that was available to help manage crises. One of the difficulties for me was the lack of information, particularly for finding out about victims. Paradoxically, I might have been as much damaged by what I didn't know. I think that attitudes on stations have also changed. The brigade today feels much less military, much less disciplinarian, more diverse and inclusive – I feel this has helped change the way firefighters are looked after following a stressful incident. There are also many more 'case-study' firefighters who are prepared to talk about their experiences in conventional media and on social media, which is an amazing step in the right direction to help break down negative attitudes to mental health.

It's hard to know whether addressing the issues surrounding Gordon's death at the time could have saved my career. Or whether his death simply triggered something in my mind that could have just been caused by events at another time. I certainly felt isolated, but worst of all, I felt, and still do to some extent, that I failed. The fire service depends on its firefighters being fit to do an operational job. Maybe if I'd had the same experience today, I'd be given longer to recover, and gradually be reintroduced to the job. But the one thing that remains the same today as it did then is that no one can predict what the next emergency call will be.

What it takes to be a firefighter is still there, buried deep in my soul. Every time I stay in a hotel, I explore the whole building, finding the fire exits, and often walk out using the stairs. When I see machines on their way to emergencies, I read the crews' body language. I know what kind of job they're going to.

Disasters have been a part of my life, and I feel fortunate to have played a small role in them. But I'm also aware of the toll they have taken.

I've had to accept that my life changed in a way that I neither expected nor planned for, and it has impacted on the stability of my relationships. I have bad days when I'm unsettled, when it sometimes feels impossible to get out of bed. I'm less able to cope with stress and sometimes take life too seriously. I shy away from attention and keep myself to myself. But I remind myself that I survived, I've moved on, and appreciate the things I have around me and make the best possible use of my time.

Perhaps I'm like one of the grey-suited old men from my childhood, but long before my time. One of those who came back from the war having seen too much, too soon, but wiser as a result. I returned from my own battle, and for that I'm both grateful and lucky.

Select Bibliography

Alleyne, R. (2009) 'Post Traumatic Stress is diagnosed far too liberally, claims trauma expert,' Telegraph website [Online] Available from: http://www.telegraph.co.uk/news/health/news/5912488/Post-Traumatic-Stress-is-diagnosed-far-too-liberally-claims-trauma-expert.html [accessed 30/06/17]

Barker, P. (1991) *Regeneration*. London: Penguin.

BBC News. (2008) 'On this Day: 1993 – World Trade Centre bomb terrorises New York City' BBC News Website, [Online] Available from: http://news.bbc.co.uk/onthisday/hi/dates/stories/february/26/newsid_2516000/2516469.stm [accessed 07/01/12].

Binyon, L. (1914) *For the Fallen: Ode of Remembrance* (first published in The Times newspaper, September 1914.)

Chambers, P. (2006) *Body 115: The Mystery of the Last Victim of the King's Cross Fire*. London: John Wiley & Sons.

Clarke, P. (2004) 'Boy murdered in row over £15 drug debt,' Press Association News, 20 September 2004 [Accessed via Nexis News database 06/11/11].

Cowton, R; Valley, P. (1988) 'Relatives angry over Tube inquest,' *The Times*, 5 October 1988, (pp unknown.)

Cowton, R; Dawe, T. (1988) 'Transport chief quits on eve of fire report; Sir Keith Bright; King's Cross fire disaster,' *The Times*, 10 November 1988, (pp unknown.)

The Daily Telegraph. (2011) 'Sir Desmond Fennell; Obituaries

- High Court judge who, as a QC, proved an incisive chairman of the inquiry into the 1987 King's Cross fire,' 6 July 2011, p25.

Duffy, J. (2004) 'Solved after 16 years – the mystery of Victim 115,' BBC News Website [Online] Available from: http://news.bbc.co.uk/1/hi/magazine/3419647.stm [accessed 16/10/2011].

Edmonds, J.M. (circa 1916) Epitaph inscribed on a memorial at Kohima Allied War Cemetery in Northern India. Via: (2001) Burma Star Association [Online] Available from: http://www.burmastar.org.uk/epitaph.htm [accessed 25/08/12].

Fennell, D. (1988) Investigation into the King's Cross Underground Fire. London: Department of Transport/ HMSO.

Fennell, D. Interviewed by Thompson, C. (14 November 2007).

Fire Statistics Monitor. (2010) *Historical Data Regarding Fire Deaths in England.* Issue 03/10 London: Department for Communities & Local Government.

Fleming, S. (1991) 'Match theory as blaze kills son,' *Ilford Recorder*, Thursday 26 December 1991, p1.

Hackney Gazette. (1990) 'Widow's stabbing shocks neighbours,' Friday 15 June, p1.

Hidden, A. (1989) *Investigation into the Clapham Junction Railway Accident.* London: Department of Transport/HMSO.

Judd,T; Clennell A. (2004) 'Last victim of King's Cross fire is named 16 years on,' *The Independent*, 22 January, p12.

Leitch, D. (1993) *A Guide to Fatal Fire Investigations.* Leicester:

The Institution of Fire Engineers.

The Living Bible, (1971) The New Testament, Red Letter Edition, Illinois: Tyndale.

London Fire & Civil Defence Authority. (1988) 'With gratitude – King's Cross fire,' *London Firefighter*, Spring 1988, pp34-36.

London Fire & Civil Defence Authority. (1989) 'The Clapham rail disaster,' *London Firefighter*, Spring 1989, pp18-23.

London Fire & Emergency Planning Authority. (2009) *How we are making your borough safer* (London Borough of Redbridge) London. 2009/2012 London Fire Brigade.

London Fire & Emergency Planning Authority. (2009) *How we are making your borough safer* (London Borough of Newham) London. 2009/2012 London Fire Brigade.

Manual of Firemanship. (1974) *Elements of Combustion and Extinction*. London: HMSO.

Metro newspaper. (2012) Wednesday 15 December 2010 'Newham Council dubbed "vain" after spending £111m on new offices' p1. [Online] Available from: http://www.metro.co.uk/news/850631-newham-council-dubbed-vain-after-spending-111m-on-offices [accessed 12/01/12].

Micheels, P. (1991) *Heat: The Fire Investigators and Their War on Arson and Murder*. New York: St Martin's Press.

Taylor, K; Hamilton, B. Interviewed by Thompson, C. (31 August 2010).

The Times. (1987) 'Lawyer to head fire inquiry: King's Cross disaster,' 24 November, p2.

The Times. (2011) Obituaries: 'Sir Desmond Fennell; Judge

who led the public inquiry into the fire at King's Cross Underground station in 1987 and whose report earned widespread praise,' 25 July 2011, p46.

St Mungo's. (2015) Rough sleeping in London still on the rise, London: St Mungo's [Online] Available from:

http://www.mungos.org/press_office/2305_rough-sleeping-in-london-still-on-the-rise [accessed 26/06/17].

Stickevers, J; and other Fire Marshals, Interviewed by Thompson, C. (26 February 1993 to 4 March 1993).

A Vision of Britain Through Time: Plaistow. Accessed 01/05/13 http://www.visionofbritain.org.uk/place/place_page.jsp?p_id=20405

Wallington, N. (1979) *Fireman! A Personal Account.* London: David & Charles.

Acknowledgements

I'm extremely grateful to Kim Hamilton (aka Kim Taylor) and Betty Hamilton for agreeing to be interviewed for Falling Through Fire – the book could never have been written without their candid, substantial and heartfelt contributions. I'd like to thank my agent Kate Johnson at Wolf Literary Services for her tireless support. Of course the book wouldn't have been possible without the guidance and encouragement of my publisher Mirror Books: I'm indebted to my editors Jo Sollis and Rosalind Powell, and to the rest of the team: Paula Scott, Fergus McKenna, Cynthia Hamilton, Melanie Sambells, Julie Adams, and Simon Flavin. The book was originally written as part of a creative writing program at City, University of London. I'm extremely grateful to everyone who has read it and provided valuable insight and feedback over many meetings, especially: Dr Julie Wheelwright, Sarah Bakewell and Peter Moore. I'd also like to thank Tony Parsons for looking through the manuscript and sharing his thoughts which was truly inspiring and motivating. I'm indebted to the late Sir Desmond Fennell QC who I interviewed, and to the writer and my friend Peter Micheels who inspired me with wise words and his books about fire. I'd like to thank Lawrence Schiller and the Norman Mailer Center whose scholarship program ensures that emerging writers are given the space and time to learn their craft. I'd also like to thank friends, family, and BBC colleagues for their support.

Finally, my story would be nothing without the men and women of the London Fire Brigade, and the Fire Department of New York. I'm proud to have served with you, and privileged to have worked alongside you.

Also by Mirror Books

The Citadel
Jordan Wylie with Alan Clark

An inspirational true story of danger, adventure and triumph over adversity.

Jordan Wylie, a young man from a tough area of Blackpool where kids like him often go off the rails, opted for life in the army. He saw service in Iraq and learned to cope with the horrors he'd witnessed, then suffered an injury that blocked any chance of climbing up the military ladder.

But an old army colleague suggested he join a security team on a tanker in Yemen. Ex-servicemen were offered dazzling salaries and 'James Bond' lifestyles between jobs protecting super-tankers. However, the price they paid was a life of claustrophobia and isolation along with the ever-present possibility of death skimming towards them across the vast, lonely blue sea. In Citadel, Jordan writes the first account of these dangerous years from someone 'at the front'. A young soldier from the backstreets of Blackpool, determined to make the most of his life, but unsure of the way forward. He found his answers in the perilous waters of 'Pirate Alley'.

Mirror Books

Also by Mirror Books

Let Me Be Frank
Frank Bruno with Nick Owens

Let Me Be Frank is the new book from one of the world's sporting greats.

A deeply personal story, Bruno talks in detail for the first time about his battle with mental illness, his time inside a mental facility, the impact his illness has had on his family and his career – and his long road back to stability.

Now ready to reveal everything about the condition that devastated his world, Frank's story offers his own unique perspective on living with bipolar disorder. His fears, his triumphs and the great affection he feels for the legion of fans he still has to this day. His aim is to give others hope and inspiration.

"Ever since I retired, one thing has stood between me and being the man I want to be. My mind. In the end it saw me locked up against my will and pumped full of so many drugs I didn't have the strength to stand. When I am in the grip of my bipolar disorder and the drugs are pickling my brain I am unable to stand for days. But I will always get back up. It is the only way I know.

"Depression comes from nowhere. From the shadows. How can you defend yourself from a punch you can't see?"

Mirror Books

Also by Mirror Books

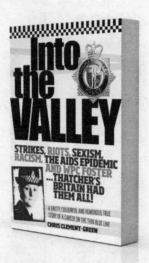

Into the Valley
Chris Clement-Green

Encouraged by the sizeable pay increase and high divorce rate,
Chris Clement-Green decided that answering a recruitment ad for the
Thames Valley Police was just the thing for a much-needed
overhaul of her life.

It was 1984, a time before political correctness, at the height of the miner's
strike and in the middle of five years of race riots. Expanding her police
knowledge and her social life, while undeterred by sexist remarks and
chauvinists, she decided to make her mark.

Chris captures the colourful characters and humour in many of the
situations she found herself in, but the job had its serious side, too. She was
at the centre of a riot in Oxford, during which her life was threatened, and
she worked with victims of rape and sexual abuse.

An often humorous, always candid and no-holds-barred memoir of a
policewoman in the 80s, this book is a personal account of a life in uniform.

Mirror Books